JESUS THE CITIZEN

BY THE SAME AUTHOR

THE SPIRITUAL PILGRIMAGE OF JESUS
    Fifth Impression, 6s net

THE HIDDEN ROMANCE OF THE NEW TESTAMENT
    Fourth Impression, 6s net

DIVINE VOCATION IN HUMAN LIFE
    6s net

CONCERNING THE SOUL   6s net

JAMES CLARKE & CO., LTD.,
9 Essex Street   London, W C 2

JESUS THE CITIZEN

BY

JAMES ALEX. ROBERTSON, M.A., D.D.

PROFESSOR OF NEW TESTAMENT LANGUAGE, LITERATURE AND THEOLOGY, UNITED FREE CHURCH COLLEGE, ABERDEEN, AUTHOR OF "THE SPIRITUAL PILGRIMAGE OF JESUS," "THE HIDDEN ROMANCE OF THE NEW TESTAMENT," "DIVINE VOCATION IN HUMAN LIFE," ETC

WIPF & STOCK · Eugene, Oregon

Wipf and Stock Publishers
199 W 8th Ave, Suite 3
Eugene, OR 97401

Jesus the Citizen
By Robertson, James Alex.
Copyright © 1927 by Robertson, James Alex. All rights reserved.
Softcover ISBN-13: 979-8-3852-4118-7
Hardcover ISBN-13: 979-8-3852-4119-4
eBook ISBN-13: 979-8-3852-4120-0
Publication date 12/10/2024
Previously published by James Clarke and Co. Limited, 1927

This edition is a scanned facsimile of the original edition published in 1927.

PREFACE

THOUGH in the last chapter an endeavour is made briefly to set the fundamental principle of the Kingdom of God in contrast with various theories of rulership, this book does not set out to be an application of Christian principles to the social and civic problems of our day. For while principles abide the same they must ever be applied by individual consciences, acting upon circumstances that are always new. Every aspect of the Divine Career has to be passed through the alembic of a separate living soul before its empirical value for that soul is established. All that this little book sets out to do is to try to make one aspect of the Career, Jesus' contact with the cities—Nazareth, Capernaum, Jerusalem—stand out for the reader from the rest a little more clearly than before. It tries to answer such questions as, How He broke through the evils in His city environment, how He responded to the call of home, what position He took as a worker with His hands,

Preface

why He was drawn into the vortex of city life, in what ways the cities reacted to this unprecedented outlook on life, and how He died at last, outside a city wall, for the difference between right and wrong.

For permission to reprint the poem on pages 157-158 thanks are due to Messrs. George Allen & Unwin Ltd.

J. A. R.

July, 1927.

CONTENTS

		PAGE
I.	"Nazareth, where He had been brought up" -	9
II.	The First Step in Citizenship	26
III.	The Home-life in Nazareth	41
IV.	The Carpenter of Nazareth	58
V.	"Capernaum, His own City"	77
VI.	Capernaum's Crowds and Capernaum's Curiosity	95
VII.	Jesus the Householder	108
VIII.	The Holy City	132
IX.	The Blind City	148
X.	The City of the Cross	160
XI.	Jesus and the City of God	176

I

" NAZARETH, WHERE HE HAD BEEN BROUGHT UP "

" No man can stand above Nazareth to-day without an uneasy, though it may be a frivolous, feeling about his destiny." Such is Renan's confession, in the preface to his fascinating but perversely wilful Life of Jesus. What is it about the town that moves the world thus to wonder ? It is the place where Christ was brought up: that alone is the reason. Sacred tradition says He was born in Bethlehem, but it was here the light of intelligence began to glow in the deep dark eyes of the little child. Here as a boy He grew, as a man He toiled, for thirty years; and He was crucified, dead, and buried before He was thirty-three. What did this town of Nazareth contribute to the unfolding life of her greatest Citizen ? Thirty years in seclusion here, and a bare three years at most in the glare of the world; one week of agony in Jerusalem, and then a cross, thrusting

Jesus the Citizen

its hideous and colossal insult to God into the gloomy sky. Nazareth, quite as much as Jerusalem, should be the holy city of Christendom.

Yet Nazareth is and has always been a commonplace country town. The ancient records call it a city; but that was the title always given to any place protected by walls. It was probably little more than a small township, out of the beaten traffic ways, and of little commercial importance. Nestling in a small hollow in the hills that rose from the plains of Ezdraelon and climbed northward toward the highlands of Galilee, the place itself had no wide natural horizons. But take the narrow stony track that winds to the top of the hill behind the town, and you see spread out before your eyes one of the noblest and most stirring prospects in the world. For centuries that great plain of Ezdraelon to the south had been Canaan's battle-ground. At the foot of the hills skirting the plain the boys of Nazareth could mark the place where, long ago on a night of falling stars, Barak and Deborah had overwhelmed the hosts of Sisera, and hurled them into the torrents of Kishon. On the east of the plain they could

Nazareth

see the hill-side where Gideon's three hundred lanterns troubled the camp of Midian in the dark, and drove the host, a panic-stricken rabble, down the vale of Jezreel and over the waters of Jordan. Nearer, on the side of Little Hermon, was the village of Endôr, where the God-forsaken Saul consulted the witch and trafficked with the spirits of the dead. Right across the plain they could see the frowning crags of Gilboa, where next day the half-mad, gigantic king and Jonathan, his son, met their mournful fate at the hands of the Philistines. That was Israel's Flodden Field over which David sang his lament for the " flowers of the forest a' wede away." As he sang he set a curse on all the life that might try to spring from that field for all time.

" Ye mountains of Gilboa, let there be no dew
 Neither let there be rain upon you, ye fields of disaster,
 For there was flung to rust the buckler of great ones."

Westward they could observe the changing lights and shadows on the gloomy top of Carmel, where, in the ancient story, Elijah, single-handed, overcame the priests of Baal in the contest by fire. They could see, too, the road where

Jesus the Citizen

" Through yon drenching thunder-blast
  Comes Elijah racing fast
  Behind, beside, before the wheel
  Of Ahab's chariot, toward Jezreel.
  Still on the rocky hillock lower
  The ancient keep, the frowning tower.
  And, where the shadows chase each other
  Down Carmel's slopes, they see a mother,
  The desperate, weeping Shunammite
  Swift from her panting ass alight,
  And clasp the prophet's feet, and there
  Unburden all her dark despair."

At the foot of that mountain mass they could see the place where the rash Josiah suffered an ignominious defeat at the hands of Pharaoh Necho and his Egyptian army. And, winding up the Samarian valleys, they could perhaps catch glimpses of the pilgrim road that led to the holy city itself. A landscape glutted with a hundred memories " of old unhappy far-off things, and battles long ago,"—the romance and tragedy of brave and glowing deeds, deeds that might bring the colour to their cheeks and the lustre to their eyes—those Nazareth boys might see from the hill behind the town. But Nazareth itself was a town without a past, without any inspiring traditions, a mere side-eddy in the stream of its country's history; and that

Nazareth

sight stirred none of its youth, save One, to dreams that moved the world.

But were they the dreams of an ardent patriotism, that stirred the soul of the young Carpenter? The only candid answer to that question is "No." In all His recorded speech there is never a reference to those mighty battle scenes, unless the sarcastic parable of the king who went to war without counting his forces is a reference to Josiah's folly at Megiddo, or unless His reference to the rain and the sunshine falling with God's impartial magnanimity on the springing fields has in it the echo of His vision of Gilboa, the field of disaster, lying in emerald radiance far below. When He addressed His townsmen from the synagogue platform, on that eventful Sabbath morning of His ministry, and drew His illustrations from His people's history, there were other tales associated with that impressive scene, tales of the prophets Elijah and Elisha that He recalled. Further, the incidents in their careers, which He remembered, spoke of God's indifference to all race distinctions. He stood on His defence before His erstwhile friends that day, and He knew that they were piqued because He had left them and

Jesus the Citizen

gone to make Capernaum His headquarters. "In carrying my message abroad to other cities, I have not insulted my native town. I love my native town. In God's wisdom I was sent elsewhere, because a prophet is never well received among his own folk. There were many widows in Israel in the days of the famine, but unto none of them was Elijah sent: it was to an alien woman in Zarepta. There were many lepers in Israel in the days of Elisha. But it was Naaman of far Damascus who received the mercy of God at his hands. O ye Nazarenes, shake off your narrow exclusiveness, your self-complacent pride ; open your eyes, open your eyes to see the wide-extended mercy of God. God is above political and national distinctions. God is not, as you fondly imagine, an almighty Jewish Zealot. God is sovereign Lord of all the world. His love and grace are not bounded by frontier marches." And His gracious words were greeted with a roar of scorn. Patriotism, indeed ! A new patriotism, this ! A fine way of showing love for His native place ! And in wrath they thrust Him forth.

And yet it is very far from the truth to say that Jesus was not a patriot but a cosmopolitan,

Nazareth

a citizen of the world. That is a false contrast. He did indeed rise above local bigotry, but none the less He was intensely patriotic. He loved His own land. When the call of the Gentile world came to Him later, as He stood on the alien shores of Tyre, He turned, and, with a look of unutterable longing toward the hills of Galilee, He said in anguish, " I am not sent but unto the lost sheep of the House of Israel." Yes, we may be sure the soul of this Nazareth Boy was thrilled by that tangled page of Jewish history spread out on the plain of Ezdraelon, not because it recorded a nation's struggle with invading foes, but because it told of the blind, pathetic fight of a noble faith for God. And musing upon the scene, now half derelict, the tall grasses and thistles growing over its wine-coloured face, with here and there a darker tangle of green beside the pools, the long reeds among the marshes of the upper Kishon shaken and sighing in the wind, His soul was filled with the sense of the futility of it all. To what had all that sacrifice of life and treasure in the plain of Ezdraelon amounted? It had not prevented the bitterness of the Exile. It had not prevented Israel being, as she was at that very hour, in

Jesus the Citizen

the hands of foreign conquerors. And in a pregnant epigram He summed His verdict up near the end of His career : " All they that take the sword shall perish with the sword." That great scene thrilled Him, not so much because it recalled the glory and the pathos of His race, but because He saw the eternal truth behind it all. Life must ever be one long heroic fight for God. The kingdoms of the earth may wax or wane ; but the Kingdom of the Lord is coming, and for its coming must His servants ever fight. Not by the war of carnage, but by the war of love against lies and hate will the reign of God be established on the earth. " My Kingdom is not of this world." It was in the light of that loftier vision that He lived and laboured and died, a patriot.

But, further, if Jesus thus rose above the narrow and bigoted patriotism of His native place, He also broke through its dark cloud of local ignorance and superstition and sin, and won His way out into the sunlight of the heavenly Father's smile. The first thing that every child learns to do is to distinguish between darkness and light. And the sensitive child dreads the dark. Jesus must have been an extraordinarily

Nazareth

sensitive child. Read the Gospels and you will be surprised to observe how often His thoughts play with the contrast between darkness and light. It runs like an undertone through all the music of His mind. Some of His parables are like Rembrandt's pictures—patches of light thrown up into vivid relief against the gloom. When He spoke of souls being cast into outer darkness, where shall be weeping and gnashing of teeth, it seems like an echo from the days of His childhood. Sweet it was in day-time to play by the fountain, when His mother went for water; and sweet in later days to run with other boys about the orchards, or to wander where "the light of laughing flowers along the grass is spread"; happier still when He was old enough to climb the hill behind the city, and view the wide prospect bathed in sunshine. But when the sun sank behind Carmel, or down into the shimmering sea, when the long shadows crept up the vale, when the narrow unlighted street became a deep trench filled with inky night, we fancy we can see the sensitive boy standing with beating heart at the door of the humble home, and peering out, and listening, with every nerve astrain, to the weird, long-drawn

Jesus the Citizen

wail of the hyenas, and to the answering howl of pariah dogs, and the moan of the owls in the outer darkness beyond the city walls—listening, and turning back with a shudder into the lighted house.

It was precisely that contrast which struck Him when He thought of the deep night of superstition, vice and ignorance that was round Him in Nazareth, where He won His way to God. Yes, in the streets of Nazareth the life was drab and sordid, like the place itself. For the city where He had been brought up was only a cluster of grey cubes of houses, and irregular, unpaved streets, with a few cobblestones for crossings, and lanes so narrow that the asses passing with their panniers pushed the bystanders close against the walls. A road ran through the town, connecting the great ways of the North with the caravan routes that passed from the ends of the earth through Ezdraelon. This was the main street, and in it stood the market-place, and on each side of it all the principal tradespeople had their bazaars and workshops. One was a carpenter's house, and through the open door the Toiler at the bench could look out and watch the market-people haggling over

Nazareth

fruit and fish and cloth and sparrows, and the children playing at weddings and funerals under the great fig-tree. And sometimes He could see a self-conscious Pharisee, pretending to be oblivious of the crowd, floating by displaying his phylacteries, or stopping a moment to lift his hands in prayer. Before He was very old He could hear and dimly understand the talk of passing merchants and camel-drivers, gossiping the scandal of Herod's dissolute court, and confused fragments of the intrigues for place and power in far-off Rome. And at the well He would hear the women wrangling, or chattering about domestic shames and sorrows, or whispering weird tales about the demon-haunted wastes, whence came the spirits that vexed them with disease.

Stay your thoughts for a moment again, to wonder at the marvel of that unsullied life. "The perfection of His purity and patience," says Principal Sir George Adam Smith," was achieved not easily as behind a wide fence which shut the world out, but amid rumour and scandal, with every provocation to unlawful curiosity and premature ambition." Not there, not there on the streets of Nazareth, but up on the hill-tops,

Jesus the Citizen

where He learned to wander alone, when the fear of this deeper darkness of scandal and ignorance and superstition banished all fear from the silence and solitude of God's kindly night—up there, alone in prayer, He broke through it all, and won His way to peace and strength and holy joy, and the whisper of His heavenly Father's voice.

One other point where this unfolding life departed from the ways of Nazareth may be noted. He not only broke through the narrow, racial prejudices of the Jew and the ignorant, scandalous life of the town, but He also broke through the cold formalism and materialistic hopes of its religion. Often He must have sat in the synagogue, listening to the sing-song reading of the law, bewildered by the dreary hedge of rules and maxims which the prosing scribes heaped around it. And when He chanced to hear a fragment from the prophets, the words of burning scorn against vain oblations, incense, new moons and sabbaths came like a breath from another world. He must have marvelled that His fellow-townsmen did not see the contradiction. But, no, the only prophetic message which stirred them was that strange

Nazareth

foretelling of a coming Messiah. This town with its inconspicuous past and its dull present, had no special prospects for the future except in such a religious dream, which they conceived in terms as crass as all their neighbours did. They were looking for a political Messiah, but not among themselves. Nobody ever suspected Nazareth of being a likely home for greatness. And nothing happened during all those thirty years to turn the eyes of the race thither. The neighbouring villages, indeed, probably just as vile themselves, despised the place. It was a dirty, disreputable town: no good could come out of it, Nathanael of Cana said. And he had lived all these thirty years only some five or six miles away. And amongst all the fragments of gossip that floated down the valley from Nazareth there were no sensational tales of an extraordinary young carpenter living there—nothing to wonder at, nothing to contradict the drab impression of the place.

No, if Nazareth herself had any dreams about the future at all, it was just this vague, religious hope—the common possession of the race—degraded and embittered by circumstance. For from that same hilltop behind the town, looking

Jesus the Citizen

northward, the Nazareth boys might often see the sheen of serried Roman spears, as the cohorts marched to and fro along the *Via Maris*. They, too, had learned to hate those unclean Gentile dogs that had overrun their land; for they heard their seniors whispering about them in the streets, with flashing looks and hissing words. They may have seen an occasional scuffle between a passing detachment and the loafing mob. For the only hint that history affords about the character of Nazareth is that it was a brawling, turbulent, obstinate place. Cudgels and stones would be used, and that was a wild game in which mischief-loving boys would delight to join. Once, perhaps, the young Jesus, standing among His companions, saw a gruesome procession, some tattered, wild-eyed Jewish rebels winding up the hillside, carrying their own crosses, hedged in by Roman spears. Some such sight must have haunted Him, until it found expression long after on the eve of His own Passion, in the words, " Whosoever will come after me, let him deny himself and take up his cross and follow me."

Can we wonder if those Nazareth boys, spying the glittering spears from their hilltop, would

Nazareth

repeat, with schoolboy exaggeration, the blustering bravado and threats of their elders, and if wishes born of resentment and hate, and fostered by superstition, became their dearest hope? "Someone is coming!" so they heard the Rabbis saying in the synagogue. It was the only time when the dreary service had a spark of interest. "Someone is coming!" They heard their parents repeat the tale in awestruck tones in the dim rushlight round the evening fire. "Did you see the sky to-night? How red it was! The cup of Jehovah's wrath against the oppressor must be nearly full. A red sky in the evening! Fine weather in the morning! The good old times are at hand again. The hated taxgatherer will have to pack and go. No more crosses on a hundred hills. The Roman triremes will carry the last of their eagles, battered and broken, far down into the Western sunset. We will have a king of our own in the holy city once again. The prophets have said it. And all the signs declare the times are at hand. Someone is coming! If only he would appear!"

And at last one day He did appear: stepped to the platform in the little synagogue—their

Jesus the Citizen

old townsman, Joseph's son, as they supposed—and they held their breath as He read, and there flowed from His lips the gracious music of an ancient prophecy: "The Spirit of the Lord is upon me, because He has anointed me; to preach good tidings to the poor has He sent me, to proclaim deliverance to the captives, and recovery of sight to the blind, to send away the crushed in liberty, to proclaim an acceptable year of the Lord."[1] And there He stopped. With deliberate precision He folded up the roll, gave it back to the synagogue steward, sat down, and paused. And there was absolute silence. At last He spoke. And the words fell like a sudden burst of sunlight through an angry sky: "This day is this prophecy fulfilled in your ears." Dumb with amazement they listened for a little longer to the golden voice, and then they rose, and with wrathful cries they thrust Him from the place, meaning to fling Him headlong from the precipice. Christ was crucified in spirit many times. This was the first of these crucifixions—His rejection by His native town. "Passing through the midst of them He went His way." A miracle, but a moral one. The enraged crowd

[1] C. G. Montefiore's translation.

Nazareth

was impotent in face of the majestic reproach of innocence. So He went His way, never to return.

If it was to-day He had come—and come to this land of ours, with all its restlessness, its vain search after things that do not satisfy, its sordid sorrows, its grim despairs, its lack of God—if He told us all our need, and offered us Himself, would we, like Nazareth, thrust Him out, nailing His spirit on a cross of scorn again? If we were to thrust *Him* out, to whom else could we go?

II

THE FIRST STEP IN CITIZENSHIP

Worship and the Church still occupy a central place in the Christian conception of citizenship. To the Jew, the assumption of the robes of manhood is ever intimately bound up with the life of the synagogue. It was always a red-letter day in the annals of a Jewish home when one of the boys became " a son of the Law." That phrase, 'a son of the Law,' means very much what we mean by the expression 'a member of the Church in full communion.' The ceremony was a very simple one. The parents announced to the ruler of the synagogue their desire that their son should be admitted to the full privileges of worship. With an exchange of courtesies the boy's name was entered on the synagogue roll, and a Sabbath day appointed when he would be called upon to take his place among the adult males. Great preparations were made for the event. New robes—the robes of manhood—with phylacteries and frontlets all complete,

The First Step in Citizenship

were purchased or woven for the boy. Never in all his school-days had he been so excited about a reading lesson as he was now about getting up carefully a certain portion of the Law. And when the day came at length, and the congregation was gathered, he was there, his pulse beating vigorously with excitement as he heard the ruler begin the service with the familiar call to prayer: "Hear, O Israel, the Lord our God, the Lord is One." The plaintive voices of the throng joined with the ruler's voice, intoning the liturgy. Their bodies swayed and bowed in rhythmic unison, like the waves of the sea. And then, when the fervent commotion had subsided, the Scribe unrolled the Law, and called upon the lad by name. He rose and climbed the bema to the reading-desk, and there before the fond admiring eyes and eager listening ears of his own relations and friends it was his great, though intensely nerve-racking and embarrassing, honour to be the reader of the lesson for the day.

Even to this day the intimacy and affection of Jewish family life is one of the fairest social relationships among mankind. We who have been nurtured in a rigorous northern climate

Jesus the Citizen

are a much more phlegmatic race; and, though we may think and feel deeply on like occasions, we make little outward sign. But in the Jewish family it was a high feast day. It was like a birthday or a coming of age. Intimates and blood-relations gathered in the house after the service, and sat down to feast. After the banquet some near relation rose and made a speech in honour of the event, praised the parents and flattered the blushing youth for his excellent appearance, and his masterly reading of the Law. And then the boy rose and made a speech, —well, read a speech (if you must have it), carefully written out, upon an ornamented and beribboned manuscript, by some village scribe, who was well paid for his composition. In this speech he told the company of the hopes he had, and the resolutions he had made, now that he had assumed the responsibilities of manhood.

The age of adolescence, the age at which the ceremony took place, was reached as early as the twelfth or thirteenth year. It was after this great event was passed that the lad could claim the right to join the pilgrim caravan in its yearly journey to Jerusalem, to celebrate the Pascal

The First Step in Citizenship

feast within the courts of the holiest building in all the world to a Jew—the Temple.

We are thinking here especially of what all this ceremony would mean to the Boy Jesus, simple, clean-hearted. The heart of youth is always full of wonders, longings, questionings. What must it have meant to a Youth brought up in Palestine 1900 years ago, amid a people who clung passionately to the conviction that there was but one God, a great unseen and all-seeing Spirit, while the alien peoples round them, and even in their midst, bowed themselves in debasing superstition before graven images? What must it have meant to a Youth taught to look down from the heights of soaring intellectual scorn upon all those false worships; to a Youth trained to believe that this great unseen God had drawn near to the holy men of His people's storied past, and whispered in their souls strange messages, which they had spoken to their country-folk; to a Youth who, as He spelt His lessons in the sacred books, heard in them, with ever deepening excitement, the echo of a sigh of longing, which grew to a rumour of hope, and burst at last into the fierce flame of a prophecy that Someone was coming, a great

Jesus the Citizen

Deliverer was coming, sent to this land and to this people from God?

Such a Youth had a tremendous heritage of story and tradition, round which all His thoughts and questionings must have turned and turned. He looked up into the eyes of His mother, that simple woman, dreamy and devout, who told Him all those stories first, who had crooned Him to sleep so softly many a time with the sweet, sad temple hymns; and in those deep, dark wells of love He read the unspoken hope that her first-born son might be this coming great one from the presence of God. *He* the promised One! Might it then be He? And as He wandered about the Nazareth hills, they became haunted hills to Him. God must surely tell Him some day. Where would be the trysting-place? He listened to the wind in the reeds down by the marshes of Ezdraelon, and its soft, healing note murmured, 'Comfort ye, comfort ye my people, saith your God.' He saw along the valleys the long, red, wavering lines of the oleanders, following the bed of some dried-up mountain torrent, and it seemed to Him a pathway where the Divine Majesty had lately passed and left the place of His feet glorious. He stooped

The First Step in Citizenship

down and looked into the face of one of these flowers, and it was far more to Him than a mere flower; it was the mysterious meeting-place of God and man, the greeting of the great Creator-Spirit to His soul.

Wandering in the folds of the hills, did He come upon some sudden patch of bright heath among the grass, and did it seem a swift smile of God to Him saying, ' In thee I am well pleased ' ? Glimpses and hints of the presence of God these were, half-guessed and gone again, wakening His soul to ever-growing wonder.

He grew like any other healthy human boy, and the deepest longing of His heart was just that great human instinct of longing after God which wakens sometime in the soul of every man. Where might He meet and be sure for ever of the presence of God ? And all that longing must have been concentrated and intensified in those solemn days of preparation before Jesus became ' a son of the Law.' What a holy book the Law of Moses was to every true-born Israelite ! With what reverence it was handled ! The Scribes who copied it did so in trembling fear, lest they should alter, even by accident, a single jot or tittle of it. Every time they had to write

Jesus the Citizen

the name of God, they first wiped the pen and took a fresh dip of ink. Whoever would handle it to read it must first purify himself with washing and with prayer. And is it not written in the *Sayings of the Fathers :* "If two sit together and exchange words of Torah, the divine presence abides between them ; and even when a single individual occupies himself with the Torah the Shechinah is said to rest upon him." (iii. 3-7). The Shechinah of God—the sacred shining of the unseen Face ! Would He see it, He wondered, when, on that solemn day so near at hand, He stood up to read the passage for the day before the Nazareth congregation ?

And now at length the day had come and gone ; the family feast was over. We may be sure He had scorned to read the set speech of the village Scribe. He had spoken His own few simple, natural sentences. He was glad to kneel at evening prayer in the quiet of the family circle, when all the guests had gone. He longed to be alone. For all day He had felt the great Presence was near. And He wanted to listen when the distracting voices of the day had died away. Yes, He had felt God with Him in that great moment when He stood up in church to read.

The First Step in Citizenship

And yet somehow the memory of Sinai, where the Law was given amid the fire that flashed about the mountain-top, made it for Him a remote and awe-inspiring Presence. Surely there must be a deeper and a more intimate vision of God than that. And then He heard Joseph and Mary talking of their going up to the Pascal Feast. He listened to the subdued, hushed tones in which they spoke about the Temple. Ah, there, every devout Jew confidently believed, the bright Shechinah—the unearthly Light of God—always rested within the Holy of Holies, or above the mercy-seat. With joy too deep for laughter He learned that He was to be allowed to join the caravan. Surely there at last He would reach the open vision of God.

Then came the excitement of preparation, the rapture of the setting out, all the wonder of the journey, the visiting of scenes made famous in His people's history, the chanting of the pilgrim songs : " I was glad when they said unto me, Let us go into the House of the Lord. Our feet shall stand within thy gates, O Jerusalem." And then at last the vision of the old grey city walls, with the great towers and minarets of the Temple, clear-cut against the Southern sky. He entered through the city gates, came under the shadow of the Temple wall, and found His feet standing within the sacred courts. It was one of the great moments of His life. Blind indeed must Joseph and Mary have been, if they did not notice, during all the feast days, that "He was absolutely possessed with the Temple, and with all He saw and heard" —the sacrificial hymns, the silver note of the trumpets, and the smoke of the sacrifice. No doubt "early every morning He was waiting at the Temple doors, and they could not get Him to turn His back on its closed gate at night." Other folk might wonder and smile. He neither saw nor cared. It was for this that He had come. And now that He was here it was the only thing to do.

The youthful Jesus, in His search for God, was representative of youth in all lands and in all ages. The world to-day is full of seekers, fuller perhaps than ever it was ; more than ever men are longing for a satisfying answer to the riddle of life, longing for the vision of God's face. And yet they are turning their backs on the House of God, turning their backs on the old ways in which their fathers walked—too grown up to sing hymns any more, too rationalistic to pray, too intellectual

The First Step in Citizenship

to listen to a sermon, too cynical to join a Church. Or they are seeking for a knowledge of God only along the ways of science, or seeking to forget Him in the gardens of to-day's lighthearted literature. They are starving their souls. The sacred words, ' Wheresoever two or three are gathered together in my name, there am I in the midst of them,' have no meaning for them.

Here at Jerusalem in the venerable shrine of His people's faith, this young Lad, who was to be the greatest revolutionary the world has ever known, the greatest heretic and iconoclast of His time, won His way home completely to the heart of His eternal Father. He never cut Himself adrift from the simple worship and the ancient ceremonies of His people's faith, even when He had broken completely with the theology of the Scribes. It was by opening all the avenues of His soul, as He lingered in the old paths of synagogue prayer and temple sacrifice, that He won His way up out of the dim twilight of our human finitude and ignorance to bask in the everlasting sunlight of God's presence. It was with a note of sad surprise and mild reproach that He answered His mother, " How is it that ye sought me all about the town ? Did ye not know that

Jesus the Citizen

I must surely be about my Father's House?" Poor and feeble all man's ways of worshipping God have ever been, alike in the days of the great Jerusalem Temple and in the most gorgeous cathedral service of to-day, yet the All-Father whose thoughts are not our thoughts, neither our ways His, condescends to meet His children there, yes, and in every place, however poor and small, where men are gathered together in His name.

But did this Nazareth Boy find the response for which His soul was longing, when His early pilgrim steps led Him to this first Passover Feast? The answer lies in those words so amazing on the lips of a boy of twelve—' My Father.' We have never thought of God in any other way except as ' Our Father which art in Heaven,' but this open secret of the unseen God has come to us from Christ. Where did He learn the secret? Everything points unmistakably to this hour. It was here, in this first visit to the Temple, that the lovely mystery, which had been slowly dawning over the sky of His soul from the days of His infancy, broke at last into the broad blaze of day. Could all those days of religious ferment and commotion in the life of the young Jesus have led

The First Step in Citizenship

to anything less than a great blossoming time in this pure, divinely gifted Soul? Why did He stay behind in Jerusalem? Why did He never seem to notice that His people had departed? Why did He never seek to follow? Two whole nights alone for the first time in His young life, where the trees of Olivet look down upon the deserted pilgrim camp. Absorbed and lost in contemplation and in prayer. Rapt in a lingering ecstasy. Utterly devoid of fear. Alone yet not alone : for the heart of the Eternal had unveiled itself within His heart, and called Him 'Son,' and He had answered back, 'My Father !'

Three short days had passed since Joseph and Mary parted with their Boy. Yet when they found Him again He was changed—irrevocably changed. Hitherto His mother had been His confidant, sharing His childish secrets. But now He had passed away from childhood : He had won a holier secret, which He could only share with God. That moment comes for every mother—a moment bitter hard to bear—the moment when the life spontaneous and instinctive in her child passes into the life reflective—a fearful, solitary moment, as Robertson of Brighton

Jesus the Citizen

puts it, when there opens on the soul an awful new world of mystery and destinies and duties, too deep and inexpressible to tell even to a parent's loving heart. That moment had come for Mary and for Mary's eldest child. This is evidently her story, kept in her heart, and told long after to the Master's followers, the bitterness and the sharpness of it not wholly withheld. Many mothers fight against the moment when it comes, and would rather keep the child than trust him to his self-found manhood. They try to laugh the growing seriousness away. One can never cajole or inveigle an awakened soul back to childhood. But one may succeed in quenching the still, small voice of God, and displacing it with the spirit of the world.

Mary learned her lesson, and hid this first sword-thrust in her heart. In any case the vision of this young awakened soul from Nazareth was too clear and sure and wonderful for any fond parental folly to destroy. And this was a moment fraught with the most tremendous destiny for the history of mankind. Here, in this Boy's experience, the barriers of sense and finitude, that separate us from the world unseen, were worn so thin that all the yearning love of God glowed

The First Step in Citizenship

through. Here He began consciously to be taken up into the very Godhead of the Son of God. So He became for the common folk of Galilee and for every honest, earnest seeker who has come into His presence since, the Transparency through whom the Eternal Father's heart is seen. Yea, so, at last upon a Cross, all the power and love of Godhead poured itself forth in that which is the very inmost secret of true Fatherhood,—self-donation, self-sacrifice that heals the world's estrangement in a great forgiveness.

Because of this great hour and all that followed it, we worship God evermore kneeling in the presence of Christ. "Wherever two sit down to meditate upon the Law, there with them is the Shechinah of God." Let us set alongside this word of the Jewish fathers, Jesus' own word: "Wheresoever two or three are gathered in my name, there am I in the midst to bless." Have we fathomed the deeps of that amazing word? Have we counted out the claim it makes? Have we reckoned up the daring? Jesus of Nazareth has superseded the ancient Law. He has become the Shechinah. He is our holy Temple flooded with all the fulness of the glory of the presence of God. Here the last and

Jesus the Citizen

highest longing of the human heart reaches up into the peace that passes understanding. He is our Priest, our Sacrifice, our God, in one.

III

THE HOME-LIFE IN NAZARETH

OF all the thirty years or thereabouts that Jesus lived on earth, it is only the last year or two that we know very much about. We know a little of His infancy, and we have one sacred glimpse of His boyhood. But otherwise concerning the thirty years in Nazareth the gospel narrative is all but silent. Nevertheless the reverent seeking heart, from a hint here and a stray word there, as the Master speaks His mind in these immortal pages, can easily construct for himself a picture of the home-life in Nazareth. And it is along that path we would seek with all humility to travel a little way now. By so doing we may be helped to see that the religion of the Nazarene, this Christian faith of ours, is not a dreamy, unreal thing, far removed from all connection with our human life, but something intensely living and urgent and pressing. And if we can discern anything of the life that was lived in those thirty hidden years, of the place this humble Artisan

Jesus the Citizen

took in the life of His family, of the hardship and poverty He endured, perhaps we will begin to see that the religion He left to the world is a religion that has drunk so deep of all the hard and bitter facts of life that it has become the only religion that has an undying and indispensable message for the soul of man.

Why is it that Jesus remained so long in obscurity? It is easy to answer that He waited till He felt His hour was come. But we must remember that He watched for the pointing of the finger of God in the happenings of the daily life around Him. And a careful reading of the Gospel story convinces us that there was something in the outward circumstances of the family which made Him certain, all those years, that His place was in the home. It is probable that Joseph the breadwinner died a few years after the visit of the Boy to the Passover Feast at Jerusalem. We never read of Joseph again in the sacred story. We read only of Christ's mother and brethren. And we see Jesus at the end tenderly entrusting the widow Mary to the care of a loving disciple. Tradition bears us out in this. There is a beautiful story in *The History of Joseph* which says that his dying pillow was soothed by the Divine Boy

The Home-life in Nazareth

whispering to him the secret of death. Just when the young Lad was beginning to take an active share in Joseph's business, the home found itself without a head one sad morning. Jesus was called, while still in His 'teens, to follow as chief mourner, the mortal remains of Joseph, to watch the great stone rolled across the mouth of the tomb, and hear it shut to with a mournful clang. And thereafter the whole care of a young family of five sons and in all probability at least three daughters fell on the shoulders of the widow and her eldest born.

Can we catch any echo of that grim struggle to keep the wolf from the door? Surely we can. It was in the hard school of the experience of those hidden years that He stored His mind with the lessons He afterwards taught to men. Many of the parables are undoubtedly early reminiscences. The scenery of them is the country-side of Galilee. And the life of them is the humble life of country people. At His own door He had often seen His mother and a neighbour woman grinding at the mill. In His own home He had seen the mother lay the leaven in the three measures of meal which He had been so proud to be able to purchase for the family needs. And, in the wakefulness of the

Jesus the Citizen

night, He had listened to the stifled commotion going on in the little barrel covered with its damp cloth in the corner. The little Boy that had asked for bread and was never put off with a stone, has no hesitation in His manhood's years in translating the child's confidence in His Nazareth parents into the man's faith in God.

And we may be sure that the life was lowly and plain even when Joseph was alive. Working people like the Carpenter's family lived in one-roomed houses mostly. A single lamp, so Jesus tells us, placed on its proper stand, gave light to all that were in the house. Surely it was a hand-to-mouth existence where one needed at times to borrow bread from a neighbour at midnight to tide over the unexpected visit of a friend. And it was a humble home where the father shared the same bed with his children. And it must have been a very little house, where he could argue as he lay in bed, with someone at the door. There is something so realistic about that familiar parable that one feels that two little ears had listened to the hubbub long ago in Nazareth. And if it was so when Joseph was alive, what must it have been when there was laid on Jesus' shoulders the whole burden of the home? How He must have

The Home-life in Nazareth

laboured and toiled to keep the roof over them, to win the daily food and clothing.

Yes, and He succeeded too, though the sweat must have often stood on His brow, and the piercing look of hunger and weariness crept into His eyes. We know how all through His ministry He hated sham and shoddy and the comfortable make-believe of the Pharisees. And we may be quite sure from that, that there was one Carpenter's shop in Nazareth where yokes were fitted so perfectly to the neck of the beast of burden as never to gall, where chairs were made to stand on four feet at once, and doors to open and shut without friction.[1] And as the people got to trust Him with their work, and the money came in, how that mother must have learned to lean on Him and look up to Him in everything ! You remember, when the wine was spent at the wedding in Cana, how Mary instinctively turned to her Boy. He had got her out of many a difficult position ; and now she told Him of the difficulty in which these poor people found themselves. And though Jesus spoke a brusque, shy, hesitating word to her, think how still she

[1] See T R Glover's *Jesus of History*, to which this chapter is more than once indebted

Jesus the Citizen

whispered to the slaves, " Whatsoever He saith unto you, do it." Could anything shed a more revealing light on the years of silence? Yes, after long experience of a thousand nameless crises in the short and simple annals of that home, mother and brethren could have said with absolute sincerity :

> " His counsels and commands so gracious are,
>   Wisest and best "

How mother and son must have grown into each other's affections as she took counsel with Him at many a little domestic crisis. Do we not read of old coats being patched till they can stand it no more, till the sewing on of a new piece only tears a rent in the old cloth? Is not that a reminiscence of the mother coming and telling her son, her help and support, that she has done her best with the garment and can do no more, and that a new one has become a positive necessity? And then do we not catch an echo of His mother's joy, calling in her friends to tell them all the outs and ins of it, when she found the coin she had lost, after much sweeping? Aye, and we seem to see a darker shadow still on that Nazareth home. Do we not read of widows with adver-

The Home-life in Nazareth

saries, of one at least with an adversary so persistent and pressing that she becomes bold, and actually plagues the callous, hard-hearted judge into granting her relief at last? Who was that enemy, we wonder? Recall that withering sentence Jesus once flung at a group of Pharisees: "Ye devour widows' houses and for a pretence make long prayers." There is that word 'widow' again, a word often on His lips. Was it not His mother of whom He was always thinking? And may not this adversary have been some pious, money-grubbing, Pharisee landlord trying to squeeze out the last penny of an unjust debt, or to sell the house over her head to get what was not his own? Human nature has not changed so much all those centuries.

Could a Man who had come through a hard experience of that sort be content with a few idle fancies for His religion? Do you think that when the Christian Church began to look on Christ as the elder brother, that when Christ Himself taught men to regard God as the Heavenly Father, they were just talking in the language of pretty but sickly sentiment? No, if we want to find the origin, the human origin, of those precious names, we will only discover it in the

Jesus the Citizen

home-life in Nazareth. That is what makes them so piercingly real, so unspeakably comforting. By the bitter experience of those thirty years, Jesus became convinced that, if men understood aright the deep, tragic meaning of the common relationships of life, they would find themselves standing in an attitude of awe and worship before the eternal mysteries of God. It is this home-life that furnishes Him with His most striking descriptions of the great facts of eternity. Let us take these two terms, Christ the elder Brother, and God the Heavenly Father, back to the test of the Nazareth experience, so that we wandering folk, who have Christ for our elder Brother and God for our Heavenly Father, may drink still deeper of the comfort of those great words.

Jesus *was* the elder brother in this Nazareth home. He was Mary's first-born son. And in His early years, as we have seen, He became the bread-winner of the home. The younger children never knew half the anguish that it cost Him to be faithful to his charge. And though the mother Mary knew much more than they, even she did not know all. Many a time He shielded her weak womanhood from bitterness, mortifica-

The Home-life in Nazareth

tion and despair; many a chill wind of human unkindness, many a sharp arrow of outrageous fortune, that might have fallen on her, He received into His own loving breast, and never breathed a word of it to them. Yet we may be quite sure that His little brothers and sisters did get to understand in their own childish way what a noble elder brother they had. They came to know what His sympathy and protection meant, and grew to love Him and cling to Him, as only a child can to a kind brother. There are few things in the Gospel more beautiful than Jesus' love for little children. One of the old Latin fathers said: "He became a child for the sake of little children."

To hurt a child was to Jesus an unspeakable thing. You sometimes hear men jest about the intemperate language of temperance reformers. Did ever any reformer use a more violent word than this? "Whosoever shall offend one of these little ones that have confidence in me, it were better for him that a millstone were hanged about his neck, and that he were drowned in the depths of the sea." We seem to hear in the passion of that word, the echo of many a time when on the streets of Nazareth He interfered with a cowardly

Jesus the Citizen

bully tormenting a child, and sent him about his business.

Recall that perfect word of His : " Suffer the little children to come to me." We sometimes miss the beauty of these sayings by not being careful with the separate words. He does not say 'suffer them to be *brought*,' but to '*come*' ; so we read it in the oldest and most authentic of the Gospels. They were actually running to Him of their own accord. He was one with whom children were always at their ease. No doubt the small members of the family found a welcome in the carpenter's shop, and strayed in to see their brother there, on their own irrelevant errands. He told them stories. And in return, many a childish secret, many a childish sorrow, many a childish confession was breathed into that patient listening ear. And it came to Him as He listened, that even so, with this childlike simplicity and frankness, must all men enter God's Kingdom.

But sometimes, of course, the little brothers forgot themselves. Do we not read also of brothers who may need to be forgiven until seventy-times seven ? He knew all about the little rebellious outbursts, and He learned that

The Home-life in Nazareth

the best, the only way to deal with the offenders was to forgive them again and again.

But, even in that Nazareth home, the elder brother had to endure at last the bitterness of being misunderstood. Towards the end of those thirty years, when His brothers were grown to manhood, He heard the call of another Voice within Him, and He began to entrust the business of the workshop to their hands. About that time they began, with wonder and fear, to watch a great change come over Him. He grew more silent and reserved. He used to wander away to the hills in the evening. And when they saw Him again in the morning, they saw the lines on His face and the mist in His eyes as though He had been wrestling all night long with some unseen spirit. When the news came, as it must often have come, into that workshop of some sad tragedy of sin, they saw His whole being shudder, convulsed with some unutterable emotion.

And then one day He left them, and they heard He had taken to street-preaching. 'The Messiah' He seemed to imagine Himself. And they said 'He is beside Himself'; and mother and brothers came to bring Him home. The world had entered those brothers' hearts, and they

Jesus the Citizen

failed any longer to understand their elder Brother. A cloud of sorrow hid the happy confidences of those early days from sight. We need not look too harshly on the conduct of those brothers. It is never easy for the brother of a despised and discredited prophet to espouse his cause, even though he may cherish a secret hope that the prophet's claim may be true. The fear of the world's laugh is strong. Nevertheless the memory of that brother's love in early years is stronger still. Years after, with Calvary between, we read that among Christ's most active followers in the early Church were His brothers. James became the head of the Church in Jerusalem. There at last is the passionate love of a youngster for his elder Brother who was so patient and tender in childhood, triumphing over all the estranging barriers of the world, blossoming into adoration and worship.

It was said of Him long ago, and it is as true to-day as ever, He is not ashamed to call us—us sinful, wayward erring folk—brethren. Earth has no greater dignity to offer than that we should be called brother by Him.

And now let us take that greatest word of His, 'the Heavenly Father,' back to the test of

The Home-life in Nazareth

the Nazareth home. Joseph died while some of the family were too young to understand, perhaps even to remember. Can we not imagine a wistful young brother coming sidling shyly to the bench one day and saying, ' Jesus, why haven't we a father, when all the other boys have fathers ? ' And when Jesus answered, ' But, my boy, you have a father,' and the little one would ask again, ' Where is he ? ' the elder Brother would say, ' God is your Father.' How that elder Brother leaned on God, as He drove His plane to earn the daily bread. Many a day, when want stared them in the face, and mother and little ones turned anxious eyes on Him for help, He went to His Heavenly Father with the family's distress. And the answer always came. Perhaps in His early years He was sometimes sent by His mother timidly to borrow a measureful of meal, when the chest at home was empty. Did the compassionate housewife take the little measure from His hands, and not only fill it, but press down the meal in it, and shake it together, and heap it up till it was running over ? Never except by a woman could measure be so tenderly insulted. And did He muse on it on His way home and thank His heavenly Father ? " Give

Jesus the Citizen

and it shall be given unto you, good measure, pressed down, and shaken together, and running over shall men give into your bosom." Surely that confident word is the result of some such experience. 'Shall not your Heavenly Father clothe you—feed you?' were not the words of a man brought up in comfort and ignorant of hunger.

Many a time, doubtless, He denied Himself that the others might be fed. Yet so near did He live to God that through all the grim reality of the daily struggle He became convinced that not a sparrow falls to the ground without the Heavenly Father. Not a sparrow! Those little guttersnipes of the bird world. The poor man's supper. Two for a farthing in any market in Galilee. He had bought them often for the home. Yet God is Chief-mourner when they fall. And many a rash and desperate cry God answered, though not quite in the way asked for or expected. Yet His soul soon discovered that the unlooked-for answer was the right answer. His faith always kept Him open-minded and ready to be corrected. He saw earthly fathers, though evil, knowing how to give good gifts to their children, and He became sure

The Home-life in Nazareth

that the Heavenly Father knew how to give the best gifts, and always gave them.

And what are the best gifts? He who knew best has told us. He says, ' Blessed are the poor in spirit for theirs is the Kingdom of Heaven. Blessed are the pure in heart for they shall see God!' The best gifts are the Kingdom of Heaven and the vision of God. But who is sufficient for these things? Christ alone was ever lowly-hearted enough and pure enough to attain to these best possible gifts in the best possible way. But to us erring men He has pointed out another way by which we can receive those gifts; and that is the way of forgiveness. Thanks be unto God for His unspeakable gift! Forgiveness is just heaven, just the vision of God, only as seen and received by the broken-hearted. When the prodigal came dragging slow, hesitating steps homewards, was it not heaven to him when the old man kissed him? The story of the prodigal son is no doubt a Nazareth incident. What village, what city street on this sad earth of ours has not its story of a prodigal? One morning it was all the talk of Nazareth that the wild young son of a certain man had disappeared from his home through the night. Jesus heard it, and

Jesus the Citizen

saw the old man's devastating grief, saw him on many a night at the end of the village street, looking wistfully along the great highway that led to the noisy city

" Where age loathes age, and youth doth youth decoy
  With pleasure's joyless travesty of joy,
  Where sin and death with linked arms walk the street,
  And night's mad heart doth beat, and beat, and beat."

Perhaps he saw him turning as darkness shut the landscape out, and heard him murmuring to himself, ' But he will come.'

And then at long last he saw the old man's hope fulfilled. He saw him begin to run, saw the arms outstretched and waving, heard the thin, distant shout of joy. He saw the father fall on the stranger's neck and kiss the soiled, battered, worn-out wanderer. And as Jesus turned away, we can imagine Him murmuring, ' Much more shall your heavenly Father.' But He knew that the joy was born out of an awful pain; knew what it cost a father's love to kiss that stained, estranged and broken creature. And He felt how much more it would cost the pure heart of His Father God to forgive. Yet He never doubted God was equal to it. Yes, much more, much more shall your Heavenly Father.

The Home-life in Nazareth

It was the anguished love of the bereaved and lonely Father God, brooding over His desolated home, that woke at last in the soul of Christ, and drove Him out along the roads that lost souls wandered, the grim and awful roads that led to Calvary. When I stand beneath the shadow of that Cross I seem to see the arms of the Father God stretched out—dumb, yearning, beseeching—speaking in a way too terrible for words the forgiveness that His love has wrought for us. There is nothing more certain in our lives than our need of forgiveness. There is nothing more real and sure in heaven or earth than the Father's offer of it to us. " Him that cometh unto me I will in no wise cast out."

IV

THE CARPENTER OF NAZARETH

The question, 'Is not this the Carpenter?' (Mark vi. 3), is the only direct hint we have as to how Jesus spent the eighteen years of His life between boyhood and manhood. Even this amount of information is grudged to us by the other evangelists, for Matthew substitutes the phrase 'the carpenter's son,' and Luke the phrase 'Joseph's son,' forgetful of their own early chapters. Nevertheless the Gospels do not leave us altogether destitute of evidence that this was the trade He followed.

Perhaps 'builder' or 'constructor' is a truer translation of the Greek word than 'carpenter'— a worker, that is, in stone and clay as well as wood. His most important tasks would be the building or repairing of houses. There was not much fine wood-work about a Jewish house or its furniture. So, as Jerome tells us, His lesser tasks would be the making of ploughs and yokes and spades. Wheels were not common in that

The Carpenter of Nazareth

land where mule-panniers and camel-backs were the usual means of transporting goods. The only familiar wheeled object apart from the mill-stone and the windlass would be the Roman chariot, a foreign importation.

We discover a good deal if we let our memory go over the story once again with these facts in view. The wise builder builds his house on a rock foundation, not on sand (Matt. vii. 24 ff.). The sane house-speculator gets an estimate from his ' tektôn ' (constructor) before he sets about building (Luke xiv. 30). The figure of the rejected corner-stone (Ps. 118) had an intimate appeal for Jesus (Mark xii. 10). There were no windows to repair, but holes in the wall had to be built up where thieves had digged through to steal (Matt. vi. 19) ; and barns were sometimes pulled down and built bigger (Luke xii. 18). The barn figures a good deal in Jesus' pictures (Matt. vi. 26, xiii. 30), in the yard where the hen called her chicks for protection as He passed. ' A door ' is an important, a mystical thing (John x. 1-9). We read of a gate or door that is very narrow but leads out into a wide landscape (Matt. vii. 13). And is there not one parable at least which takes us right back to the carpen-

Jesus the Citizen

ter's bench—the humorous picture of the man with the plank in his eye trying to fish the splinter or speck of sawdust out of his brother's eye (Matt. vii. 3 f.)? Do we not read also of work done in green wood and in dry? (Luke xxiii. 31). And of heightening things by cubits—or trying to plan how to do so (Matt. vi. 27)? And in one of the Logia recovered from the papyri found at Oxyrhynchus, we read, "Raise the stone and there thou shalt find me: cleave the wood and there am I."

Then for the Nazareth housewives there would be an occasional new or mended meal-measure, or dough-trough (Matt. v. 15, vii. 2, xiii. 33; Luke vi. 38), there would be oil-cruses or lamps to make, shaky lamp-brackets to fix (Matt. v. 15). And for the farmers there were yokes and ploughs (Matt. xi. 30; Luke ix. 62). And turning to the parable of the man who planted a vineyard, we find a touching proof of the trade our Lord pursued. He borrowed the plot of the parable from Isaiah, but, in the most authentic account of it we find nothing of the heart-breaking labour of gathering out the stones, and nothing of the careful selecting of the vines. Jesus tells us only that the owner built a paling round his vine-

The Carpenter of Nazareth

yard, that he dug a foundation for a wine-press, and that he built a tower in the vineyard. These are the features of the work in which a builder would be interested.

It is true He drew His great symbols from Nature rather than from human artifice. But He was a lover of Nature. And it is like Him to be more engrossed in the anxieties and troubles of the humble agricultural folk for whom He made implements than in His own activities— to have a sympathetic ear for stories of lost sheep, and disappointing soil, and spiteful neighbours who came in the dark and sowed tares, and wolves ravaging the flocks; and to have a helping hand also for the poor beast fallen into the pit. No doubt also there was a garden attached to the home in Nazareth, where young eyes might watch the green buds coming on the fig-tree and hear the older people say, ' The summer is at hand '; where Joseph may have showed the young lad the tiny mustard seed, and told Him to watch for the blade and the great bush by-and-by, in the spot where he sowed it; where bad boys may have promised to do some weeding yet stolen away to play, and sulky boys refused to do it, yet afterwards may have gone.

Jesus the Citizen

Possibly there were slack times in His own occupation, when He hired Himself out as a day-labourer, or took a spell at the harvest when the hands were scarce, and the ripe corn clamouring for cutting. According to tradition His mother's father was a sheep-farmer near Sepphoris a few miles north of Nazareth. What finer holiday for a boy than to be out with His grandfather's shepherds on the hills?

There is a fanciful theosophical school which thinks that the hidden years were spent with the Essenes and that He was their shepherd.[1] But there is nothing helpful in the suggestion. There is hardly a reference in any word of His to any distinctly Essene doctrine. And we have also to remember that tradition says Joseph died before He was nineteen, certainly long before the days of the ministry. And if Joseph died thus early, then the other boys were too young to support the home. And the young oldest-born had to do the fathering. Every Jewish father had to train his child from early years to a trade, and very rarely was it anything but his own trade. Yes, surely Jesus was the

---

[1] cf Moore's dull story with the fine beginning, *The Brook Kerith*

The Carpenter of Nazareth

carpenter: that was God's clear call to Him in those hidden years. "He went down with them to Nazareth and *was subject* unto them."[1]

These years at the bench were the years of the Divine apprenticeship. They were what many a soul, soured because of ambition thwarted, would have called the lost years of His life. These were the years which the undiscerning neighbourhood pointed to with scornful wonder, and said, He that is commonplace let him be commonplace still. They mocked at the absurdity of the Carpenter becoming the Prophet. They were offended at the presumption.

Man looketh upon the outward appearance. For eighteen years they had gone in and out of the carpenter's shop, and seen Him chipping and chiseling, smoothing and fitting wood. He had sweated like other people. His hands had grown hard and horny—the hall-mark of the commonplace. 'We knew His mother well,' they said. 'And His brothers, James and Joses and Simeon and Judas. Yes, of course we have not forgotten

---

[1] One feels in looking over these details, and comparing them with the greater nature-pictures of the parables, that in the case of the former they slip out casually, unobtrusively, spontaneously into His speech, whereas in the latter the artistry is deliberate and conscious It may be an indication that the former belong to a more intimate side of His life than the latter

Jesus the Citizen

them. His sisters are all living here in this town still—ordinary people like ourselves. What right has He to pretend to be different ? The upstart presuming to be better than the class from which He sprang ! Indeed the virus of class-consciousness is no modern growth. Jesus sought to lead simple people to a new view of life, and He was rejected by Nazareth, as every other leader has been, around whom the least suspicion has grown that he has risen above his class. There is an Indian proverb which says ' Every lamp has a shadow beneath it '; and what misleads a man's own people is that they will persist in creeping into the shadow, and so fail to see the light that streams out beyond it. How could a man who carried a carpenter's kit or a mason's tool-bag be a leader of men ?

Familiarity breeds contempt, we say. We are too much under the sway of proverbs, which are generally only half-truths. The trouble about this one is that we always think the contempt is justified. We never think that familiarity can have made any mistake. Familiarity breeds contempt, but what is it that breeds familiarity ? It is too often the low tone of men's outlook upon men and things. Familiarity breeds con-

The Carpenter of Nazareth

tempt because what breeds familiarity is itself so often contemptible. In what narrow and mean horizons public opinion often lives and moves and has its being! When a man makes a slip we say, '*Now* we are beginning to see what he really is.' Men are ready enough to believe that the worst of a man is the truest thing that can be said of him. But a sudden revelation of greatness or goodness where it is unexpected—that is altogether another matter. Men's eyes are so accustomed to the gloom and the straws where they exercise their muck-rake that a sudden glance at a flash of compelling glory blinds them. They fail to see the crown held over their neighbour's head, and they refuse to believe it is there, or refuse to believe he has any right to it. Familiarity destroys men's insight and discernment, while all the time it persuades them that the very opposite is the case: it creates in them the bias, the prejudice that they cannot be surprised by anything in the character of one they have known long and closely. The Messiah come? What, the village carpenter!

But God looks upon the heart. How little we really do know of each other! We see the foam and the froth, the flotsam and jetsam rushing

Jesus the Citizen

by on the surface of the stream. Down into the deep, dark waters of the soul we seldom see. These Nazarenes, who gossiped beside the bench, knew the routine of this Man's life: that He rose early and worked steadily and conscientiously: was clean-living, honest, and straight. What of it? Did they not give Him credit for it? A good man—quiet, simple, natural, unassuming member of society—everyone admitted it. He was fond of children, and flowers, and birds, and beasts. He was given to fits of silence. Used to wander after work hours on the hill-tops. But they just shook their heads, and smiled, summing it all up in one word which always satisfies the gossiping mind—it is so eminently illuminating—' Queer ! '

Somehow they respected His opinion. His judgment, they could not help admitting, was always wise and sane. They no doubt often remarked, ' Yes, that is just the right word to say about it.' But they made the remark with an entirely self-satisfied air, as if that was exactly what they themselves would have said. They forgot that there are some things that are obvious only after they are said. But there were a hundred other things that entirely escaped their attention.

The Carpenter of Nazareth

They did not notice how the Man grew silent when their gossip became particularly vulgar and empty—or perhaps they did sometimes, though it only gave them a passing spasm of annoyance. They did not understand the quick flush of shame when some sordid scandal was turned over by them; they did not see the lips drawn tight and bitten hard in pain, when some tragic tale of sin or sorrow was brutally analysed and dissected by them; they forgot the sigh, the half-stifled cry of prayer, the tear that sometimes stole down His cheek—they knew not whence it came nor why. These were dim glimpses and broken fragments of the real events that were taking place in His tremendous soul; and they missed all their significance.

But it was all clear to God. It was part of God's destined plan for this village carpenter, that those waves of spiritual commotion should sweep over His soul among the chips and the shavings, the motes and the beams of that Nazareth workshop. It was the Divine apprenticeship. For in those eighteen years the soul of Christ was moulded, sharpened and refined till it was made the perfect instrument, yea, the vessel into which the heart of God Himself

Jesus the Citizen

was poured in the blood-red wine of passion, pain, and death for human sin.

It was all wrought out on a very humble plane. But meet the tests of life there successfully and you can meet them anywhere. He could join in the children's innocent games, but He was never known to jeer away an idle hour in ribald talk or empty folly. He could speak a kind and gentle word to the soiled and outcast men and women of His native town, but he was never known to compromise His character by frequenting the haunts of shame. He knew the pain of hunger, but never once descended to a shady deed: He could look the whole world in the face in noblest independence. The men of Nazareth never saw what greatness was being wrought out on this lowly scale. Nevertheless the soul of flawless faithfulness in the things of low degree is the soul that alone is truly ready when the great occasion comes. And the man, whom men respected in a patronizing way for his self-forgetting goodness, becomes our hero when, at the call of duty, he lays down his life for another, becomes—oh, not at the time, long after—our Saviour, our Helper sent from the hand of God, when His life goes out in darkness for the sake of

The Carpenter of Nazareth

a sinful world. The Carpenter? Yes, but the very Son of God.

It is only when we turn to those later years of the ministry that we learn the secret of the Divine apprenticeship. The world to-day knows in its rough and ready way what God's design for the Man of Nazareth was, what was the purpose He had planned for Him to do. He was calling Him so to become the servant of the human race, so to spend and be spent, so to efface Himself, so to give Himself up body and soul for the need of men that when they really and honestly came face to face with it all at last upon the Cross, they might be constrained to say with broken hearts: 'That was the love of God for me.' And that was the burden of His message when He spoke to the men of His native city in the synagogue that day. Yet with amazed and irritated scorn they asked, 'The Carpenter?' ... If we had been in Nazareth that day, would we not have shared their judgment? If God had really called the Man to such a tremendous task, would He have allowed Him to waste eighteen years of His life making ploughs and yokes and spades? For such sublime service, we would have thought, there must be a far more noble, a far more fitting and adequate training. But the wisdom of God makes foolish the wisdom of men. What essential difference is there between the Divine apprenticeship and the Divine task to which He was called? Because He was called to obliterate Himself for the world's need, He was bidden to suppress Himself through long years of patient drudgery for the sake of a poor and humble home. Yonder in the wilderness, at the beginning of the great Career, He met and overcame His great temptation. The baleful light of an evil spirit beckoned Him to take a short cut to the conquest of the world, the way of self-assertion and display. Sternly and deliberately He chose the long, lonely way of sorrow, gloom and death, by which alone the world could be truly won for God: and He did it in the strength of the eighteen hidden years.

Think on all the amazing features of His character. Does it not strike us, as we read His life, what an air of quietness and confidence there is about Him, what serenity and self-possession? We are too familiar with the impatience of the young reformer, who thinks he has a commission to put the world in order. But Christ waited for God. His patience is amazing

The Carpenter of Nazareth

—till we remember that in those years of obscurity and silence He learned to know God His Father, and man His brother, so well that the goal of His life grew to noonday clearness before Him.

Think again of His austere reserve, His self-restraint and self-repression. How great He is in His very silence! No man could be thus silent who is driven ignorantly toward an unknown destiny. See Him at last before Caiaphas, and before Pilate. That is the world's sublimest example of the powerlessness of circumstance to humiliate—the one scene in all history of which humanity has most reason to be proud. Can this be the Carpenter? Yes, and it is those years of self-supression that have blossomed at last into that towering majesty of Divine reserve.

Think once again. What is it that lies behind His serene confidence, His patience, His silence and reserve? He calls it " my peace "; and it was the peace of a perfectly surrendered will to the purposes of God. It is because of the perfection of His obedience—not of constraint, but of a completely dedicated and consecrated life—that His death on the cross has redeemed life from being a comedy of the gods, and turned it into a revelation of the love of God for men.

Jesus the Citizen

Have those eighteen years nothing to do with this obedience? "He went down with them and came to Nazareth and was subject unto them." And by the devotion of His attention to the little country orders of a little country business, He has made every lowly task of life for ever grave and honourable and sacred. But more, far more. It was because He learned the lesson of obedience so perfectly in Nazareth that He became fit for the supreme obedience, the devotion of His life to the carrying out of God's great plan for mankind.

We, too, are all here at God's invitation. It is not we who have thrust our little lives into His world. God has brought us here—called us into life for a purpose. And He trains us in a long apprenticeship. Life is often full of commonplace, and monotony, and weariness, and stagnation. Day after day comes to an end, and we can point to no lasting achievement. At home, the housewife rises and dusts day after day; to-morrow there are always the same places to dust, almost, one is tempted to believe, the same dust to remove. And so the weary round goes on—round and round like straws whirling in some side eddy of the meandering stream;

The Carpenter of Nazareth

sowing and reaping, reaping and sowing, buying and selling, selling and buying again, making and breaking and mending and re-making; and no end ever seems to come in sight except the inevitable one of the last long silence—with which our efforts have nothing whatever to do, unless it be as a vain attempt to stave it off a little longer. And it is hard, terribly hard to believe that we belong to the world's grand army, enlisted to effect the designs of God. But then we remember that commonplace bench at Nazareth : the world's Redeemer day after day drudging away at building and repairing houses, at making and mending the homeliest articles of daily use till He was thirty years of age. Then three short, troubled years at His Divine vocation; and then the life snuffed out on a felon's gibbet. And we have not the least doubt that among the crowd flocking back through the gates of Jerusalem at the end of the gruesome spectacle, voices were heard to say, " He was only a carpenter. He thought Himself to be somebody. His life was all a confused and pitiful mistake. And yon is the swift and tragic end of it."

Blessed be God we know differently to-day. We know that the crucified Nazarene has filled

Jesus the Citizen

the world with a worshipping host, that multitudes have died for His cause ; that His name has covered Europe with mighty cathedrals and even in the remotest glen reared a house of prayer ; that He has inspired the world's mightiest victories for freedom; that He then bore and is still bearing the sins of the world; that His sacrifice still burns and glows in the heart of humanity and

> "Love and sorrow still to Him may come,
> And find a hiding-place, a rest, a home."

Aye, weariness and drudgery and insignificance may come and find their meaning, hope and solace there. For the measure of our worth to God is not made by the lowly circumstances of our probation, our apprenticeship; but only by our faithfulness.

Further, life may be lowly and obscure, it may have a shorter or a longer probation—stretching even, it may be, from the cradle to the grave—nothing apparently but a long struggle to keep soul and body together, and then life sinks in darkness, and our friends may wonder why we were born. Let that Life that ended on a cross be to us the key of promise. It looked so futile on Calvary. For surely it is one of the most

The Carpenter of Nazareth

inspired thoughts of Saint Paul when he suggests that He who lived the life of a builder in Nazareth still lives the life of a builder, in Heaven. God not only fits our apprenticeship for our vocation on earth, but when He calls to higher service, He gloriously transforms our earthly vocation. Think of that great unseen temple, the building of God not made with hands, whose stones are the lives of believers, and whose building is to go on and on till God has made the pile complete. Who is the builder of that unseen temple of life? Under God it is the living and exalted Lord. Do we perpetrate an extravagant fancy when we suggest that the thought goes back in loving and reverent recollection to the earthly Jesus, the Builder of Nazareth? As on earth in the hidden years, so in eternity, is His vocation, only immeasurably enhanced and glorified—a Builder.

Do we doubt and hesitate? Standing in the Temple courts in Jerusalem, where He had faced the sceptic Sadducees, and passionately constituted Himself the guardian of the people's hope of Heaven, did He Himself not predict His victory, and the victory of all the faithful over death, in one sentence so arresting that His accusers trumped it up against Him when he

Jesus the Citizen

stood before the High Priest's chair ? " Destroy this temple, and in three days I will build a temple not with hands." Was this not the enduring temple He was to raise, when the ancient shrine of Jewry was levelled to the ground, and all the sacrifices of slain beasts had passed for ever away ? Was it not this house of God not made with hands, in whom we also are builded, built upon the foundation of the apostles and prophets, the Builder Himself being the chief corner-stone, which other builders, vainly building, had despised ?

V

" CAPERNAUM, HIS OWN CITY "

Nazareth was the cradle of Christ, but Capernaum was the cradle of Christianity. In Nazareth the light of Truth was kindled in the soul of the youthful Jesus, but it was in Capernaum that the light began to irradiate the world. The place ' where He had been brought up '—that is the glory of Nazareth ; but to have been called ' His own city '—surely Capernaum's is the more enviable glory. Of Capernaum may the prophet's word which Matthew recalls most truly be spoken : " The people that walked in darkness have seen a great light, and upon them who sit in the region and shadow of death the light sprang up."

It must not, however, be imagined that Christ's first sight of Capernaum was when the call of God brought Him down to the Lake to begin His ministry there. The Lake of Galilee was an easy day's walk from Nazareth. And only five miles from Nazareth Mount Tabor thrusts itself

Jesus the Citizen

into the eastern sky, conspicuous and detached, offering a challenge which no youth of spirit could refuse. And from its domed summit more than once He must have gazed eastward, down into the great deep trench where the Jordan runs, and seen the blue waters of the Lake spreading themselves out seven hundred feet beneath the level of the Mediterranean.

" Clear silver water in a cup of gold,
  Under the sunlit steeps of Gadara,
  It shines—His Lake—the Sea of Chinnereth—
  The waves He loved—the waves that kissed His feet
  So many blessed days   Oh, happy waves!
  Oh, little, silver, happy sea, far-famed
  Under the sunlit steeps of Gadara."

All that Jesus saw from Tabor's summit ; but He saw something else which the modern eye alas, can no more see. He saw round the lip of the Lake an almost unbroken girdle of gleaming city walls. For in those days Galilee was a land teeming with human life and activity. The historian Josephus would have us believe that into that small area of a hundred square miles there were crowded some three million inhabitants. Even after due allowance has been made for the bias and exaggeration of that partisan Jew, the

"Capernaum, His own City"

population must have been great indeed. And the centre of its abounding activity was the shore of this little inland lake; and Capernaum, perched near the most northerly point on the shore, was, as it were, the heart where the surge, the beat, the rush of all this life could be most distinctly felt. When Joseph, the carpenter of Nazareth, took the young Jesus down to visit the scenes by the Lake, Capernaum would undoubtedly be the goal of their journey. True, the great new city of Tiberias, midway along the Lake's western shore, was nearer. But it was an alien city, built by the Idumean Herod, with elaborate Greek and Roman architecture. It was stocked with foreigners. It was rendered obnoxious by the presence of Herod's dissolute and luxurious court. Worst of all, it was built on the site of an ancient cemetery. The mocking king had ruthlessly disturbed the dust and bones of the dead. The town was unclean. No pious Jew of the time would think of entering it.

Yes, Capernaum was the centre of attraction. Did not all the great trade routes from the south and west, from Egypt and the Mediterranean converge on Capernaum, gathering themselves there into one great road, which ascended northward over the shoulder of the hills, and by the upper reaches of the Jordan, striking out at length beneath the shadow of Hermon, and across the desert to Damascus? Capernaum, they would say, was the place, with its thriving vineyards and cornfields in the fertile plain of Gennezareth which stretched along the shore between it and Tiberias. Capernaum was the place, with its fleet of boats and its prosperous fisher-folk, its fishmarket, its bazaar, its customs and exchange offices—this frontier town with its Roman garrison, captained by that large-hearted centurion so popular with the Galileans, so interested in their Jewish faith. Had he not built them a synagogue whose white walls (if we accept the evidence which the pathetic ruins offer to-day), rising conspicuous among the houses of duskier basalt stone, were the glory of the town? Busy, bustling, self-important, self-satisfied Capernaum, with its fifteen to twenty thousand human souls, nay, more than self-important, "exalted to heaven" in its pride—that is the Master's own description of the place.

Yes, this was the city which the country Lad sometimes visited in the company of Joseph, for the Nazareth family had relatives living there.

"Capernaum, His own City"

And as the still, observant Boy paced by the strand, and listened to the measured risp, risp of the little waves falling on the shingly beach, He could see glimpses of inland Chorazin, a few miles further north through the trees, and Bethsaida (Fishertown) close at hand along the shore. He could see the cliffs on the east side of the Lake, with their crown of cities, Gadara and Gamala, Aphek and Hippos. He could let His eyes travel south along the whole extent of the Lake, until they rested on the cloud of smoke that hung over stinking Tarichæa, with its fish-curing factories; then up along the western shore, past Hamath, an ancient health-resort, with its hot, medicinal springs, to the towers and palaces of abhorred Tiberias; nearer still, Magdala, cursed into vice by its propinquity to that dissolute city, and then, possibly, little Dalmanutha, gleaming among the fair green gardens of Gennesareth. Who will venture to measure the stirrings in the heart of the youthful Jesus as He beheld that moving scene? As He grew to manhood, many a time He must have gazed towards that teeming Lakeside from the hills near Nazareth, and felt strangely drawn to it by an impulse He could not well explain. The face of the crowd had deeply moved Him, and

Jesus the Citizen

perturbed His soul. But when the clear call came to Him at last from God, He knew the meaning of that nameless unrest. It was the wistful eyes of God He had seen, looking out into His, through all the emptiness and heartache and restlessness of mankind. Where else should He begin to unfold His God-given message, if it were not down there, where the ends of the earth seemed to meet—yonder where He could see, packed into one intense and concentrated picture, a mirrored reflex of all the world? That was why Capernaum became 'His own city.'

There is a familiar proverb to the effect that God made the country but man made the town. And there is of course a certain truth in the epigram. Amid the scenes of Nature's beauty and sublimity, looking up to the rocks and snows and far-off summits, or down on the green wonder and gleaming waters of the valleys, where life and growth speak their parable of beneficent mystery, and even the mystery of death has its awful loveliness—there amid the brooding silences, the magic conjuring of cloud and sunshine, and mists that trail their phantom shapes like frightened ghosts across the moonlight, it is easy to believe that all

"Capernaum, His own City"

that mingling glory and terror are the warp and woof of the living garment of God. But God is not so obvious in the town.

What after all was the life which confronted Jesus in Capernaum, when He made His new home there, and later occupied a humble lodging in Peter the fisherman's home? It is specially true of a Jewish city that the distant view is the best. Just as we, looking up from the surface of this earth, so racked and torn with sin and strife, towards the white stars in their distant purity, find it hard to believe that life on their surface can be sordid and vile, so the young Jesus, looking down from Tabor on the far-off glitter of Capernaum, may have dreamed chiefly of the wonder and majesty and strength of the current of human life that was borne through its streets. But when "a spirit in His feet" led Him at last within its walls, startling must have been the disillusionment. Like all Palestine cities, its streets were aggressively wayward, ancient and unfinished in appearance. Here and there were wide spaces where tents were pitched, where camels and mules were tethered; and everywhere the noise and colour of the Eastern crowd. Confined within the city walls, the narrow lanes,

Jesus the Citizen

made narrower in the daytime by the provision stalls of the merchants, till there was scarcely room for passing beasts of burden, seemed more like tunnels than streets; for the houses, forced upward for expansion, made the sky of the town-dweller but a thin strip of blue seen between "lofty precipices of stone." The cobbled way beneath the feet was filthy and untidy. The inhabitants had a characteristically Oriental lack of sensitiveness to smells. And the sordid litter of odds and ends probably did not distract their eyes from the fine buildings that rose out of it. Everywhere could be heard the strident haggling of bargain-makers, and the shrill talk of men and women. Publicity and comfortlessness seemed to be the two outstanding marks of city-life in Palestine.[1]

Our Lord Himself knew well how a secret whispered in the darkness of the dwelling-room, if spoken upon the flat roof-top, where people went to rest and bask in the sun at mid-day, speedily became the property of the town, for at least ten roof-tops were within ear-shot of each one (Luke xii. 3).

---

[1] See Dr Kelman's article on Palestine (Dictionary of Christ and the Gospels) to which this chapter is indebted for some of its details.

" Capernaum, His own City "

As Jesus passed, He must have noted that the people's interests were petty and trivial ; and that the tone of the town was low. Here were some angry fishermen like to come to blows with the tax-gatherer ; and there some wily camel-drivers trying to slip their goods past duty free. Here were some vinedressers grumbling about the drought, or hiding their self-seeking under the guise of a spurious socialism, affirming that they had as much right to the products of the vineyards as their masters ; there the poor slaves murmuring because they had so little bread to eat. And in the evening the day-labourers coming in from the fields, muttered fiercely about being unjustly paid. He marked their fondness for litigation too, how they haled each other before the law-courts upon the most trifling pretext. And He noted the obsequious hypocrisy of the Pharisee, how he fawned upon the Roman centurion and called him ' Euergetes ' (benefactor). Poverty and luxury lived shamelessly within sight of each other. Lazarus with his sores was laid at the gate of Dives ; the pariah dogs sniffed at him as they passed. And there was the notorious case of the miser who owned so much of the rich corn lands of Gennezareth, who builded his new barns

Jesus the Citizen

and openly boasted that he was independent of the smiles or frowns of Providence, and who was suddenly struck dead in the night. All the things we call modern vices, older really than the days of Noah, were there. And as Jesus passed through it all, and saw the poor folk in the bazaar buying a few sparrows for a frugal meal, pity and humour must have mingled in His heart as He said to Himself, ' Even so like these sparrows, the cheapest thing in the market, the souls of men and women are cheap in the brutal world to-day. Yet there is none in all this teeming crowd beyond the Heavenly Father's pity. *That* is absolute. Even those little sparrows come within its ken.'

And when we strip our modern civilization of its few distinctive outward marks, have the conditions of life in the city changed so very much? Has the so-called Christian civilization of our day made it any easier to find God in the town? Row on row of godless brick and mortar, the heartless pavement stretching on and on interminably, the insignificant individual lost in the indifferent crowd, the monotony of it all, throngs and loneliness, uneasy pleasure, muttering poverty, restless prosperity, lurking shame. Futile, vain, without

"Capernaum, His own City"

purpose, without end seems the daily round of toil and sin and sorrow. Now as then there are the same dissatisfactions ; rich young rulers with every earthly ambition reached—all the world at their feet—and yet crying out of their deep unrest, ' What lack I yet ? ' Now as then there is the same loud clamour for more meat, more pay ; now as then there are the same grotesque social anomalies, and the same nagging friction between class and class ; now as then there is the same vague longing for some cataclysmic change of government, some revolution to alter the face of society.

And what does it mean ? Why is it so difficult to see God in the city ? Because the city has buried her soul beneath all that superficial dream which men call life. We have lost sight of each other's souls : we have little time to get acquainted with our own souls. We meet about our daily work, and we talk the surface chatter of the day, the last great football match, to-day's scene in the Town Council, last night's murder, the recent fire, the latest sensation from the law courts, the excited debate in the House. But down beneath these wandering odds and ends of conversation, beneath the surface impressions and the empty

Jesus the Citizen

chaffer, lies the city's soul. Yes, man may have made the city, but God was in the heart of man, and God is in the city, and God sees its soul.

A generation ago one would hardly have thought of quoting a great passage from one of Carlyle's greatest works. Everybody read Carlyle then. But the following lines will be new to many young eyes : " That stifled hum of Midnight, when Traffic has lain down to rest ; and the chariot wheels of vanity, still rolling here and there through the distant streets, are bearing her to halls roofed in, and lighted to the due pitch for her ; and only Vice and Misery, to prowl or to moan like night-birds, are abroad ; that hum, I say, like the stertorous, unquiet slumber of sick Life, is heard in Heaven ! Oh, under that hideous coverlet of vapours and putrefactions, and unimaginable gases, what a Fermenting-vat lies simmering and hid. The joyful and the sorrowful are there ; men are dying there, men are being born ; men are praying—on the other side of the brick partition men are cursing ; and around them all is the vast, void night. The proud Grandee still lingers in his perfumed saloons. . . . Wretchedness . . . shivers hunger-stricken in

"Capernaum, His own City"

his lair of straw. Anarchism plots in cellars, statesmen are playing their game of chess whereof the pawns are men. The Lover whispers to his mistress . . . the thief lurks in wait till the watchmen snore. . . . Gay mansions, with supper rooms and dancing-rooms, are full of light and music and high-swelling hearts ; but in the condemned cell the pulse of life beats tremulous and faint, and blood-shot eyes look out through the darkness which is around and within, for the light of a stern last morning. . . . Upwards of five hundred thousand are sleeping and dreaming foolishest dreams. Riot cries aloud and staggers and swaggers in his rank dens of shame ; and the mother, with streaming hair, kneels over her pallid dying infant, whose cracked lips only her tears now moisten. All these heaped and huddled together, with nothing but a little carpentry and masonry between them."

These are only a few sentences torn from the vivid picture of the Scottish prophet. And if the rough-hewn genius of Carlyle could thus make the godless piles of building melt away before his imagination, till he saw into the infinite abyss of the soul of the city as it moves through its dream of sin and sorrow and vanity, what must the

Jesus the Citizen

vision of the city's soul have been, when seen by Christ's eyes, through which all the insight of Divine Love looked out upon the world? Could He not see God in the city? Nay, He saw the city in God. It must have been to Him like some burning wound in the Heart of the Divine Sorrow. All that moan and surge of restlessness and discontent—like the yearning of the waves upon the Lake-shore, or like the shouting of the waters when the sudden storms swept down the glens and smote its face—was the voice of the city's empty and neglected soul, a voice distorted and embittered by the welter of that vain dream of life which pressed above it, yet crying up over it all. Nay, it was more: it was none other than the anguished call of His heavenly Father's heart, which He dared not disobey. And that was the reason why He broke at last from His quiet home in Nazareth. That was why He descended from His sunny and secluded hills down into the throbbing life beside the Lake. Think you it cost Him nothing? Why, many an abrupt and broken word, spoken about this time, seemed to be wrung from His soul: they betray the anguish of a heart torn and bleeding by the ordeal through which it had to pass. " I have no home now,"

"Capernaum, His own City"

He sadly had to say at length, " no home on earth, only my heavenly Father's home. I have no mother and brethren and sisters now save only those who do my heavenly Father's will."

"Citizens of Capernaum," He said, that eventful Sabbath morning near the beginning of the great Career, " citizens of Capernaum, vaguely longing for some earthly change of government, it is not an earthly change of Government which will cure your unrest. Behold, I announce to you a coming change of government : repent, the empire of God is at hand." . . . " Citizens of Capernaum," He said on that equally eventful Sabbath, when amid sorrow and forsaking He closed His ministry there, " citizens of Capernaum, clamouring for bread and better pay, would your hearts be satisfied though you got the utmost limits of your desire ? Nay, nay, what your hungry souls want is the love of God your heavenly Father ; and you will find it in me. I am the Bread of Life. Taste of the Bread I offer you, and hunger no more."

We do not, of course, ignore the other side of Jesus' ministry. He went about doing good. His healing touch soothed many a broken life; and lashing at many a social abuse with His

Jesus the Citizen

indignant, holy scorn, He was a conscience to the town, and righted many a wrong, while those who once profited by these wrongs gnashed on Him in impotent fury. But this was the central thing: with this He ended as He began: " No social revolution will make a single fraction of difference in your life, if your heart is wrong. Not change of empire in the land, but a change of empire in your heart—a Kingdom which is not meat and drink, but righteousness, peace, joy, love, faith: seek that first and the rest will come. Solve the problem of your own heart. Let me, the Christ, into the city of your soul. Will it do nothing to cure the world's wrong if I set the tangle and muddle of your soul right? Will it be no step in the solution of the problem of housing, if I give your cramped, deformed thoughts light and room and breathing? Will it be no step gained for your city's health if you let me cleanse away your unclean desires, your guilt and shame? Do I cast no light on the mass of unjust and undeserved poverty that abounds if I put an end to your emptiness, your hunger of heart, your poverty of spirit? Give me but a lodging place in the city of your soul, and soon all the thoughts, desires, longings, resolves,

"Capernaum, His own City"

and aspirations—the citizens of your soul—will be gathered around the door, and I will lay my hand on them and heal them all."

The world has not yet learned Christ's message. And the unsatisfied heart of man, whether in poverty or comfort, is crying out for some new social Utopia, calling Christ's vision of a Kingdom of Heaven a quixotic dream which the grim facts of to-day have shattered. Nevertheless His ideal for the world is the only reality. For let us remind ourselves that there is no real change of heart unless it leads presently to full sacrificial service and effort to heal the social wrongs. Social service, even more than the cultivation of the inner life of the soul, should be the true end and aim of all the moral activity of the followers of Jesus. Indeed, every noble heart that is trying to heal the social evils of its day is working at least from the motive of love of humanity. And that always has and must have, whether consciously or not, all the love of God behind it. Jesus' basis, the heart changed and directed by the love of God, should be the ultimate foundation of all efforts for the uplift of humanity. Without that, the noblest political Utopia ever planned will be crucified, schemer

Jesus the Citizen

and all, upon the Cross of the world's selfishness, and mocked and flouted and flung with laughter down the wind. "Come unto *me*," said Jesus, " come unto me all ye that labour and are heavy laden and I will give you rest."

VI

CAPERNAUM'S CROWDS AND CAPERNAUM'S CURIOSITY

Let us for a little join the crowd on the streets of Capernaum. We have seen how Christ was drawn by the city crowds; let us stay to see how the city crowds were drawn by him. Christ was master of the crowd. He "was able," as one writer has expressed it, "to put his ear to the ground, and hear, below the babble of business, the sighing of hearts that needed God." He could read "the look of the streets" as no man has ever been able to read it—with imagination and tenderness, and reverence and deep desire. The crowd absorbs most of us. We are each just another drop in the stream that flows along the pavement—jostled and pushed, glanced at and instantly forgotten, ourselves equally careless and unconcerned. The man of imagination—the poet or the novelist—may be able in some measure to abstract himself from the crowd. But even so he is only an onlooker.

Jesus the Citizen

The orator finds that the crowd reacts on him like an exhilarating draught; the reformer may sometimes be able to catch a glimpse down into the still dark waters of pity and sorrow, love and hate, courage and despair, that flow beneath the frothy surface dream. Much more deeply was Jesus of Nazareth affected by the crowd.

It was not the crowd in the mass, but the separate lives of the individuals that compose the crowd that He saw. He looked into the faces of men as they passed, and plainly read the stories of their lives. Here was a wrinkled brow, and thin, worn, eager look and hurrying step—a tired heart driven by sore compulsion or craving, on and ever on. Here was a face of shadows, shadows about the brow, shadows about the haunted eyes—a weary conscience burdened with memories from which it fain would escape. Here was a radiant face, bright eyes and lips that hummed the fragment of a song, because the heart knew that somewhere the flame of happiness was lighted by the hearth and love was beckoning home. Here was a pale face with thin lips drawn tight and stern, a dauntless will fighting its last fight with cruel fortune. That sob of someone passing was the involuntary confession

Crowds and Curiosity

of a breaking heart. That sigh spoke its own story of loss or longing or regret, in a soul that was made to 'look before and after and pine for what is not.'

He knew the daily heroism of the poor, and how the strong man hungry yields his last morsel to his fainting, needier neighbour. He knew the nameless courtesies practised among the lowly, how the compassionate housewife heaped the little measure full of borrowed meal for a needy neighbour's child; how a man would lend a loaf at midnight in a friend's emergency; and how one woman would help another at the grinding; how a father's heart would bleed if his son asked for bread and the crust was meagre; how neighbours hurried to help to raise a fallen beast out of a pit; how they laughed and chattered with kindly joy over the finding of a strayed sheep or a lost sixpence. He knew the touching chivalry of poor men and women who seek to shield the nakedness and hide the shame of their still less fortunate comrades. The image of God marred and distorted and broken could still be discerned by the eyes of infinite love beneath veils of dim resentment and suspicion, behind the clamour of the market

Jesus the Citizen

and the roar and din of trafficking. But He could also see the emptiness, the ugliness, the awful need of God that lurked beneath the painted mask of mockery and mirth. And so the city crowd was drawn to Him, because so He drew it to Himself with the cords of love. It was deep calling unto deep.

And yet at first the crowds assembled to listen mainly out of curiosity. That was what happened in Capernaum, that eventful Sabbath, when He stood up before the multitude assembled in the hall which was their court-house and council chamber and place of prayer in one. The place was full; for the commander of the Roman garrison, who had lately erected the building, and was himself a devout proselyte of the gate, had made the attending on the reading of the law a fashionable thing on the weekly rest day in Capernaum. But who was this? Who was this? So unlike the rabbis who read the law, and with their cold casuistry and legal hair-splitting, with their piling-up of precedents, had spread over the sky of heaven a weary weight of parchment, shutting out God. Who was this who so disturbed the conscience and moved the heart to wonder; who calm, serene, convincing,

Crowds and Curiosity

spoke in His own authority, and His words went home, and could not be evaded or gainsaid ? Who was this, that with burning sincerity and pleading love seemed to be rolling aside that parchment, and showing us again the loving heart of God ?

And then a strange thing happened: in the growing excitement the place became tense and still; and suddenly a poor epileptic shrieked his hysterical protest; and then that ringing voice, throbbing with power, won its way through the dim confusion of the jangled nerves and soothed the troubled mind to peace and sanity. Can we wonder that all that evening, ere the sun was set, they followed Him through the streets, bringing their broken bodies to be healed by Him ? They pressed on Him, hanging upon His words, hearing His message with a half-discerning wonder, breaking into incoherent joy. And then in the darkness came that unprecedented scene, when the tired Man withdrew to Peter the fisherman's home. What a picture it is of deep-moved curiosity: " all the city was gathered about the door " ! Far into the night that surging, excited mass was clamouring there, eager for a sight of Him, pouring out their tales

Jesus the Citizen

of individual wrongs and woes, asking Him those puzzling questions which all the ingenuity of the Rabbis could not explain, calling on Him perhaps to settle their family quarrels, summoning Him to be their leader in a revolt against the oppressive burdens of Rome.

Such was Capernaum's curiosity. Was it anything more? Was the soul of the city mob anything more than half-awakened from its dream of life? How did Jesus receive their advances? Within the dim-lit room He sat, His friends wondering at His stillness, His brow furrowed with disappointment, His heart sore. Far into the night He sat, sleepless, brooding, long after the cries of the crowd had died away into silence, and they had gone, leaving the street deserted. And then, rising when it was yet a while before dawn, He stole out alone into the darkness, and passed up from the lake-side far among the enfolding hills, and spoke His heart out into the listening peace of God. Yes, it was only curiosity, not thirst of soul, that drew the uncomprehending crowd. That scene around the door on that first Sabbath night of His public ministry in the synagogue was typical of the excitement that followed, when the news of the

Crowds and Curiosity

new Prophet and His pleading for a renascence of faith spread like fire round the Lake, was carried by traders up to the fish-markets of Jerusalem, and borne by the caravans into the uplands of Galilee by the Way of the Sea and over the Jordan into the Decapolis. The questions with which they plied Him that night were doubtless the questions with which He was assailed till the close of His career, now by the fury of the Scribes and Pharisees, and now by an undiscerning mob whose excitement would have burst into the flame of rebellion, had He yielded the slightest countenance to their urgent desires. They were questions about poverty and charity, about ceremonial and ostentation in religion, about sickness and calamity, about taxes and Sabbath-keeping, about politics and daily bread.

He knew how it would end at last, how the clamour would reach a crisis, and how, when He finally refused to respond to their worldly hopes, the excitement of the city would spend itself, and the curious crowd would melt away. And so He stood one day, months after, by the Lake listening again to the ceaseless falling of the waves upon the beach, catching again a glimpse of inland Chorazin through the trees,

Jesus the Citizen

and facing Bethsaida close by along the shore; and all that spectacle of human activity seemed to melt from the scene before His sorrow-laden eyes, and He lifted up His voice and spoke a solemn prophecy: "Alas for thee, Chorazin! Alas for thee, Bethsaida! For if in Tyre and Sidon had been wrought the deeds I have performed in you, long ago, in sack-cloth and ashes, they would have repented. Verily for Tyre and Sidon it shall be more tolerable than for you. And thou, Capernaum—up to heaven wouldst thou be exalted? Down to Sheol shalt thou be flung!" Because thou hast enjoyed the greater privilege of light, thine is the more awful responsibility. Because thou hast impatiently flung it away, thou thyself shalt be flung away!

That was over 1900 years ago. And to-day what is the scene that greets the traveller's eyes beside the Lake of Galilee? There is but one town there—a poor, fevered place of but five thousand souls—and three or four clusters of squalid mud hovels, round the whole extent of that desolate shore. And that one town is Tiberias—the abhorred Tiberias! The inhabitants of Capernaum held it up to derision, and doubtless said, " Tiberias will have its swift

Crowds and Curiosity

short day. All the life of the Lake is gathering here. Our town will be a glorious city, exalted to heaven some day." How grim the irony of time! Bethsaida, Chorazin, Capernaum, where are they? Vanished utterly. They have been indeed brought down to death. The *savants* are still quarrelling about their exact location. It is pathetic to think that one of the likeliest indications of the site of the place that was called His own city is in a name which the natives still give to a heap of tumbled ruins, *Khan Miniey*. It means "the lodging place of the sorcerer." What Christian piety has failed to preserve the bitter execration of the Jews has done. To-day the lizards play among the ruined walls, where the maiden-hair fern grows so luxuriously. There is a tangled wilderness of scrub, where the fair gardens of Gennesareth used to blow. There is scarcely a single boat to break the monotony of the Lake's expanse. Its waves now beat upon an abandoned shore, sighing out their music of a mournful might-have-been.

Was it a baleful curse the "Sorcerer" cast upon the city which He called His own? Ah, no, if we translate His words, not "woe unto you," but our homely Scots phrase: "I am wae for you,

Jesus the Citizen

Bethsaida, I am wae for you, Chorazin," far more nearly conveys the Master's emotions as He uttered the doom of the cities. The cities have gone, not because He cursed them, but because the insight of His wounded love carried His vision far into the future, and He saw the end of a slow-moving, natural law. With all the longing of His heart He wanted to win the cities. That was why, though He loved the sense of freedom, the beauty and the big horizons of the open country, He always returned with daylight to spend Himself in and upon the city.

And He made an extraordinary impression on the cities. He always does. Dimly the great soul of a city feels, for it never really understands, that Christ is in some way the beating heart of the Divine Reality for which it yearns. But Christ does not save cities. He does not save men in the mass. He only saves individuals. The city mob surges after Christ for a nine days' frenzy of excitement, and then is gone. And standing in the light of our Lord's prophetic foresight, may we not see the same slow-moving, natural law at work to-day? No city on earth is eternal. Some day perhaps when new stores of Nature's powers are tapped, and facilities

Crowds and Curiosity

of transport perfected, and greater freedom of access won to the land, there will be no cities, but all the sons of toil spread out in lesser communities over all the land. And may we not catch a hint of the Master's mind in the solemn fulfilment of His prediction? Should the state of things continue where Christ needs to save, in the midst of such heart-breaking poverty, and temptation that badgers and persecutes with its effrontery? Not that the idea of a city is wrong, not that the existence of the city is a sin. The soul of man is a city: that is why the environment he tends to make for himself is the throng and rush of a city. And according to one scripture God is going to gratify that impulse of man some day, in a heavenly city, a new Jerusalem, "a city that hath foundations, whose builder and maker is God." But in the cities of earth, man is the victim of his own environment; in the country man is surrounded with the environment of God. And there is always something diseased and abnormal and unreal in the environment man makes for himself; —some reflection of his own brokenness, something which must be destroyed if man is to be saved from himself. Standing in fancy by the

Jesus the Citizen

desolate shore of the Lake of Galilee to-day, may we not say of Bethsaida, Chorazin, Capernaum, sadly but tenderly, " all their sin and sorrow and misery are done away."

And may we not lift our hearts in gratitude to God, because the desire of the Master's soul drew Him down into the teeming activity of the Lake-side—because God did with a piteous eye look upon Capernaum? For, if He did not save the city, think of the individual souls He blessed, and won for citizens of the New Jerusalem. Think how a pagan soldier, puzzling his unaccustomed mind about faith in an unseen God, came through his tender-hearted concern for a sick slave, to learn at last what it meant, at the feet of Christ; how a poor paralytic of the town, distressed and weeping about the sins that wrought his helplessness, as they lowered him through the roof to the Master's feet, heard, as in a dream, from mortal lips, words that could be said by God alone: " Thy sins are forgiven thee." Think how Jairus, his love overcoming his pride, became a sharer of the mystery of everlasting life; or how the woman that came so far to touch the hem of His garment for her sore disease, shines for a moment in Capernaum's

Crowds and Curiosity

street, a drop from the ocean of suffering, radiant in the light of the Master's smile, and goes home the possessor of undreamed-of joy. Think how a handful of simple fisher-folk, leaving their broken nets for His sake, became the catchers of a multitude whom no man can number, of souls for God. Think of that little lad, whom He set in the midst. The simple, unquestioning trust of that child, has done more for the world's weal than all the commerce of Capernaum. Think above all of Matthew, the despised and insignificant taxgatherer, who became the first evangelist, to whom we owe the preservation of so many golden words of Jesus. He went up from his unclean money desk, with its constant round of bickering and deceit, up from the life of nameless oblivion, along the road that led to Jerusalem, to help to win the kingdoms of the world with Christ. Simple souls, humble lives, but lighted by the immortal light of the Master's friendship.

VII

JESUS THE HOUSEHOLDER

THESE words once fell from the lips of Jesus: 'If they have called the Master of the house Beelzeboul, how much more them of His household.' It is not our purpose to deal with the special occasion concerning which the words were uttered, nor yet to speak of the main thought of the words themselves. We recall them now simply because they contain two phrases which send the mind wandering wistfully over all the days of our Lord's ministry, searching for an answer to some eager questions of the heart,—'the Master of the house,' and 'those of His household.' Jesus here describes Himself as a householder with a family of sorts. Did Jesus have a home—a home of His own—during the days of His ministry? We ask ourselves the question because we long to know. We hope there may be a common sympathy with that desire. For there are a great many people who deprecate this hankering after the lowly

Jesus the Householder

details of the Lord's career. They think it is not treating the Lord of Glory, the Saviour of the world, with becoming reverence and respect. Scornfully they ask, What has it got to do with the destiny of our immortal souls? We are not afraid of that scorn. Jesus spoke the great facts of eternity in the homeliest pictures of our earthly life. It is in stooping to share the simple facts of our humanity that He reveals to us the deepest and loveliest secrets of God. And what is the noblest fact of human life? Most of us will agree that it centres in the word 'Home.' We do not mean the four walls of a house: a man may sometimes make the place where he eats and sleeps his hell. We mean the crowning glory of human life—God setting the solitary in families. Home in that sense is a holy thing, the one temple that has endured through all the ages of mankind. If there is nothing like it in heaven, then heaven is a poor and empty place, with no attraction for the heart-hunger of man.

But heaven *was* Home to Jesus, nothing but Home—Love—a Father happy among His children. He translated all His good news into the earthly language of Home. Surely

Jesus the Citizen

it cannot be wholly a vain question to ask whether He founded a home, and what it meant to Him. Had He no home, no house of any kind, no fixed place of residence while He went about doing good ? The Gospels have not told us definitely of this. We think of Him most frequently as the homeless One, the Wanderer whom God never set in a family of His own. He Himself once said in grim and sorrowful irony that He came to be the breaker up of homes. " I am come to set a man at variance against his father, and the daughter against her mother, and the daughter-in-law against her mother-in-law. And a man's foes shall be they of his own household." That last sentence, as we shall seek to show, was spoken out of the bitterness of a personal experience. Yet we will dare to say this : He became homeless in order to make Home the last sure reality to the soul of man.

But the facts are not so simple as that statement seems to make them. Let me invite you to look at these facts, for we shall find in them, for all their mingled tragedy and pathos, cause for deep wonder and gratitude and joy.

We know that He made the city of Capernaum His headquarters during the first two years of

Jesus the Householder

His ministry; and it is, of course, the years of His ministry we are concerned with here, not the early home of His youth in Nazareth. What was the nature of His place of sojourn in Capernaum? For there is no doubt about it: there was a roof-tree of some sort to which He ever and again returned. When He came back from His first Gospel tour in Galilee, the word passed through the town, 'He is home!' (Mark ii. 1). Does that just mean 'He is back to Capernaum'—the city that His friends who gave us the Gospels call 'His own city'? Literally the words mean, 'He is in the house.' And these words are not alone in the Gospels. After He set apart the Twelve Disciples in the high lands above the Western shore of the Lake, we read that they returned home (Mark iii. 19). And we get a glimpse of them all together, Master and disciples, trying to eat a meal disturbed and interrupted by the insistent clamour and movement of the crowd outside. Not a very restful picture of home truly, but once more the words are "in the house." And on yet another occasion, when He had spoken to the crowd some memorable parables in the open-air, we see Him entering "into the house" with His

Jesus the Citizen

disciples, and circling round Him, as He sits there, they ask Him for an explanation of one of these parables. Was He a householder then in Capernaum, as the phrase 'His own city' would suggest?

There is a verse in the Gospel of John which, in a measure, lets us into the secret. We read that 'after this'—after He had returned from the preaching of the Baptizer at Jordan, after the wedding at Cana—'He went down to Capernaum, He and His mother and brethren and His disciples" (Jn. ii. 12). This must be history pure and simple. Nearly every fact is translated into symbol in this Fourth Gospel, but there is none here. And there can be only one explanation of the precise detail. They were leaving the old home in Nazareth permanently behind them. There is no mention of His sisters going with Him. Does that marriage in Cana mean that He had just seen the last of His sisters settled in a home of her own? Recall the words which the townsfolk whispered to each other when He revisited Nazareth some time after and spoke in the old synagogue where He had worshipped as a boy. They said, " Is not this the Carpenter, the son of Mary, brother of James, and Joses, and

Jesus the Householder

Simon, and Judas? And His sisters"—note what follows about the sisters—" are they not all here with us?" Surely these questions not only corroborate the word in John which says that only the mother and brothers went with Him to Capernaum, but also they help to confirm the suggestion that it was to establish a new home in Capernaum they went. Perhaps He had handed over the business to a sister's husband in Nazareth, and trade was too meagre in the little highland town to maintain them all. Certainly it was not to support Him in what they considered His preaching craze that the brothers went with Him to the busy city by the Lake. Down in Capernaum, one cannot but believe, He still plied His trade in manly independence, building and repairing houses, mending boats and fittings of the caravans that halted at the customs house, making ploughs and yokes and spades for workers on the land. Doubtless it was in the open yard of the workshop, while His hands were busy, that His teaching first began.

Alas! in a few brief months His life in the new homestead came to a tragic end for Him. Behind the reticence of the Gospels about His home-life there—and indeed, it seems to us, explaining that

Jesus the Citizen

silence—this tragedy lies half-concealed and yet revealed. We have quoted one of the revealing words already—' A man's foes shall be they of his own household.' Let us mention some others. "A prophet is not without honour, but in His own country, and among his own kin, and in his own house," is surely a revealing word. And there are words which may reflect the resentment and bickering of His own brothers. "Whosoever is angry with his brother without a cause shall be in danger of the judgment, and whosoever shall say to his brother Raca shall be in danger of the council," and so on. There are also words which speak of the right attitude for the offending brother to assume : " Therefore if thou bring thy gift to the altar, and there remember that thy brother hath aught against thee, leave there thy gift before the altar, and go thy way, first be reconciled to thy brother, and then come and offer thy gift." And this saying, not recorded in the Gospels : " Except thou look on thy brother in love, it is sin." And there are words also which express the true attitude of an offended one to his brother : " If thy brother shall trespass against thee, go and tell him his fault between thee and him alone : if he shall hear thee, thou hast

Jesus the Householder

gained thy brother. But if he will not hear thee, then take with thee one or two more that in the mouth of two or three witnesses every word may be established." And the great word about forgiveness of a brother : " I say not unto thee, Until seven times, but until seventy times seven." These words show how deeply the thought of estranged relationships between brothers had occupied the mind of Jesus. They seem to reflect personal experiences of His own.

It was after the choosing of the Twelve that the final break with the family took place. The second brother James was also a deeply religious man. From the description which early historians give of James in his later years, it is almost certain James had earlier become a Pharisee. He must at least have been so in spirit, if not in name. A Pharisee and a religious revolutionary living side by side in the same home ! Surely there are the makings of tragedy there. The Epistle of James, which contains an epitome of James' teaching, is richly strewn with echoes of the talk that fell from Jesus' lips beside the bench in Capernaum. Phrase and sentence again and again remind us of golden words which we find recorded in the Sermon on the Mount and else-

Jesus the Citizen

where in the Gospels. But James heard them with a hostile and censorious heart, there, in Capernaum. The old conventions of the Jewish faith still held him fast. And apparently the other brothers were in secret sympathy with James. Possibly they resented the invasion of the home, when Jesus brought the chosen Twelve, fishermen and tax-gatherers, unclean folk! back with Him and tried to entertain them while the crowd clamoured about the door. Certain it is that as they watched the growing crowds beholding His deeds of healing, hanging on His words with wonderment, and as they listened to the scornful officials of the Temple saying, ' He is in league with the devil : it is the power of Beelzeboul,' doubt, alarm, suspicion and mistrust entered the breasts of the family. Love and confidence were driven out. Home became an empty name to Jesus. And at last one day, surrounded by the eager crowd down by the shore, His passionate words pouring from His lips, He saw them—mother and brothers— supported, nay, urged on by some malice-loving Scribes, pressing in on the outskirts of the throng, and He heard the excited voice of James say, ' We must take Him home: He is beside Him-

Jesus the Householder

self: He is mad!' 'See!' said someone of the crowd to the Master, 'your mother and your brethren want you.' We have read the words that follow many a time, read them lightly and unthinkingly perhaps, read them in lively tones as if they were an epigram, or gravely as if they were a piece of cold philosophy, or sternly as if an indignant rebuke. The truth is, every syllable of them is a drop of blood. "Who is my mother? And who are my brothers?" asked the quivering lips. And then we are told He looked round and round on them which sat about Him. The memory of that look never faded out of Peter's mind. It is due to him we have it recorded in Mark's Gospel. It was laden with anguish, shame, yearning, sorrow unutterable—a long hesitation while the call of the blood, the love of family, the ties of home tugged and strained at His heart. And then they broke! Thrusting out His hands— the only time we are ever told of a gesture of the Master's hands while He spoke in public, and the gesture means surrender, committal— thrusting out His hands, in an abrupt, swift movement towards His followers, He said, 'Behold my mother and my brethren. For

Jesus the Citizen

whosoever shall do the will of God, the same is my brother, and my sister, and mother.'

That was enough. Mother and brethren understood, and turned and stole away. And as they went, the ears of James, stung to alertness by the smart of the rebuke, caught the sad words like a knell of doom, ' I say unto you that every idle word that men shall speak they shall give account thereof at the day of judgment.' James had called his brother mad. An idle word ! A cruel word ! Worse than the thrust of an assassin's sword; and not the first by any means. You think that to say James heard this reproach of Christ is only fancy. Read the Epistle of James again, read the third chapter. Surely there is the record of James' belated remorse. What is the sin upon which he harps and harps ? The sin of the idle word. ' The tongue, the tongue, it is a fire, a world of iniquity. It defileth the whole body, and setteth on fire the course of nature; and it is set on fire of hell. . . .'

What is the meaning of this poignant scene in the Gospels ? It means the separation from His kinsfolk by Jesus. But think, for a moment, why. It was because home, the home He knew

Jesus the Householder

and loved, had lost its value, lost its reality for Jesus. Coldness and estrangement, envy, strife, had displaced love. Home was in ruins, was no longer home for Him. But why did He in effect renounce it? Why did He make Himself homeless? It was in the interests of a holier ideal of Home. ' Whosoever shall do the will of God, the same is my brother, and my sister, and mother.' Note the two words that end the saying, the last to fall from His reluctant lips at this time—' and mother.' Yes, He had to say them, but it cost Him a terrible effort, the effort of a son's breaking heart. It was only a temporary break with His mother, as we know from the tender word spoken from the Cross; but it had to be until His work was done. " Whosoever shall do the will of God "—these were the ones that claimed now the undivided love of His heart. So in the very moment when He had rendered Himself homeless, He constituted His new family under the open sky. Love, His love for them, and for all who do the will of God— that was the bond of His new family, His new home. He became homeless for the sake of Home, for the sake of the true ideal of home. He became homeless that we men and women

Jesus the Citizen

might learn to take God with us into our homes and make them homes indeed.

But was this the end of the career of Jesus as a householder ? Let us go back to the words at the beginning of this chapter: ' If they have called the Master of the house Beelzeboul, how much more them of His household.' They were, we believe, spoken long after this day, though they are an echo of the very scene we have just recalled. Still He calls Himself Master of the house, though He never went back home. Is it only a metaphor now upon His lips ? And when we turn to scan the records again, we find that at the very end of His two years in Galilee, after the rupture with the scribes and Pharisees over the washing of hands, He enters into the house, that is to say, His home. And the disciples are there questioning Him in consternation about His indignant words. ' In the house ' ? Had he then a hired room ? Or was it a room lent Him by a friend ? He had plenty of friends in Capernaum by this time. He had cousins there, and two of them were disciples. The devoted excise-man, Matthew, entertained Him once; and Peter the fisherman had him sometimes to a meal and even for a

Jesus the Householder

night's shelter and rest. Was it a room of Peter's, who had seen the breaking heart writing the story of its anguish in that look when Jesus relinquished the home ties? Did Peter now offer to make Him an inmate of his household? There are two facts which help us to answer that enquiry. In the very last days that Jesus ever spent in Capernaum, when He returned from Cæsarea Philippi, the great decision made to face the cross, we read once more that when they entered ' into the house ' He asked His disciples what they had been disputing about along the way. Striving for places in the Kingdom! And He crowned His gentle rebuke by a beautiful action parable. He lifted a little child and placed him in their midst. Then gathering him in His arms He spoke still further from this living text. The presence of that child in the house is enough to show that this was no house of Jesus' own. He shared a roof with another family now. Tradition says that this child was Peter's son.

One other incident immediately followed, which seems to make the proof complete. They were not very long home, before the temple-tribute collectors called at Peter's door. They came to remind him that owing to his absence

Jesus the Citizen

from home his payment of the sacred tax had fallen into arrears. 'And what about Jesus?' they asked. 'Does He not pay this tax?' And Peter, embarrassed, for his purse was empty, answered, 'Yes.' 'Go down to the harbour, Peter,' said the gentle voice behind him. 'You will catch a fish, and it will fetch a shilling. That will pay for me as well as for you.' It was the exact amount of the double tax. And this matter concerned Peter's household alone, and Jesus was involved. Yes, clearly Jesus was an inmate of this home. But there is one more inference from this story which we cannot pass by. The tax, one fancies, could hardly have been levied on the minors and dependants in each household. If Jesus had been merely a dependant, living temporarily upon Peter's bounty as a guest, He would probably never have been challenged about paying His dues.

Does it waken no thrill of satisfaction in our hearts to discover that Jesus insisted upon paying His own way? Right to the very end of His Galilee days, He maintained His independence, His self-respect. Absorbed though He was in His Divine calling, He must still live the life of a true man in the world. He will owe no man

Jesus the Householder

anything but love. Perhaps He had perforce to change His occupation when He gave up His home. Sometimes, one fancies, He became a gardener—the vocation of the land-worker recurs so often in His parables ; sometimes He may have toiled in the boats with His friends on the Lake. And then in His own hired room in Peter's house—that upper chamber on the roof, to which He needed no lodger's key, for an outer flight of steps led up to it—there He would break bread with them in the evening, and speak reverently of the Kingdom which was Home. He was ' Master of the house,' and they were His children, His household.

What celestial nights these must have been ! How He tried to be a father to them in spiritual things—yes, and a mother too ! For He knew the human emotion which He has described in the homely figure of a hen gathering her brood beneath her wings. Home love is a cherishing, fostering love. How He lavished His love upon these friends of His—and in the most intimate, homely way ! He had by-names for some of them : 'Peter'—the rock; 'Boanerges'—the two hot-heads. Matthew—God's gift—was the name He gave to Levi. One of the three Judases He

Jesus the Citizen

called Lebbaeus, ' my hearty,' or Thaddaeus, ' my cheery one ' ; and another He called Thomas—the Twin. ' Little Flock ' He called them all. In graver mood He called them ' brothers ' ; in lighter vein He called them sometimes ' children,' sometimes ' lads.' But we think His favourite word for them was ' little ones '—a cherishing love indeed.

And home-love is a defending love. One of the few times He ever was angry was when Pharisees found fault with the disciples for sitting down to food with some of the grime of the nets still on their hands. To save them from mortification, He would dare defy the most powerful ecclesiastical authority that ever held sway among men. And how deep is the chivalrous indignation that breathes through the terrible words, ' Whosoever shall offend one of these little ones that put their trust in me, it were better for him that a mill-stone were hanged about his neck, and that he were drowned in the depths of the sea ! ' Verily a defending love. Thus He fulfilled the rôle of ' Master of the house ' to them of His household.

It was a wonderful time for them. And all too soon it ended. The paying of that Temple-

Jesus the Householder

tax was practically the last act He ever performed in the fulfilment of His obligations as a citizen and a householder. It was probably only a few days after this that the grim, sad words were spoken: "Foxes have holes, and the birds of the air have nests, but the Son of man hath not where to lay His head." Once more, and finally, the household is broken up. He is a homeless Outlaw, roaming the hills and the valleys. Why? Why did He take this drastic step, denying Himself the comforts of a dwelling? You will find the reason, spoken on the shores of Tyre a few weeks before this day, when He made His great decision to win all His people for His Heavenly Father's Kingdom, or die in the attempt. It is all summed up in the great phrase, laden with a patriot's pity and deep desire: "the lost sheep of the House of Israel." He became homeless for the sake of the wanderers from home. It was the vision of His Heavenly Father's sorrow-riven heart brooding over His desolated Home that drove Christ out along the ways that led to Calvary. The call of His heart through all the streets and lanes of that great Passion Journey is still the call of the risen Christ to wandering men and women:

Jesus the Citizen

"You've gone astray
   Out of your way,
Come home again, come home again!"

"It is not the will of your Father in heaven that one of these little ones should perish." Yes, He became homeless that He might call the wanderers home.

Shall we follow Him for a moment along that road where He wandered homeless for a year, towards Jerusalem? Did He give up His independence when He resolved to surrender His privileges as a householder? We do not believe it. We are told of some women of means who followed Him from Galilee to Jerusalem ministering to His comforts. There are times, doubtless, when He would have gone hungry, had it not been for their devotion. But we know that the disciples had a common purse; Judas Iscariot was their treasurer; and the money was not all spent when the last night of the Saviour's life on earth was reached. It did not contain much. The thought of spending ten pounds, to feed five thousand, once brought them to the point of consternation. But it was in the main sufficient for their common wants. And assuredly Jesus' savings

Jesus the Householder

would be there in that purse along with the rest.

Many of His nights, we doubt not, were spent in caves, and in woods beneath the open sky. When He let His disciples try to find a hospitable roof to shelter them on inclement nights, they miserably failed. A Samaritan village would have nothing to do with them, and they were mortified and angry. And henceforward Jesus had to undertake that task Himself. Everywhere along the road we watch His amazing gift of making friends. Even a ruler of the Pharisees entertained Him, somewhere near Tiberias, we fancy, as He travelled down the Lakeside.

Think of the mothers in that town beyond Jordan bringing their babes to receive His farewell kiss and blessing. Could there be a more entrancing revelation of the place He had made for Himself in their homes? Think of the scene on the streets of Jericho, when across a sea of disapproving faces He shouted His winsome, resistless self-invitation to the home of the little despised tax-collector in the sycamore tree: "Hurry up, Zacchaeus! Down you come! I am going to stay at your house to-day." That was how He always made His way. What

Jesus the Citizen

could His disciples do in face of that amazing power of instantaneous friendship, but just leave it all to Him?

Think again of Bethany. "A certain woman named Martha welcomed Him to her house." It was not the disciples who had won an entrance for Him to that home. He had stolen the hearts of all that family. Back He came, again and again in these closing days, to this quiet retreat. It is the most homelike scene in all this homeless year. Or think of the man with the water-bottle waiting at the gate to show Peter and John the upper room in Jerusalem where He was to eat the last supper with His disciples. "The Master saith, 'Where is *my* guest-chamber?'" Clearly that was a secret arrangement beforehand between Jesus and some friends of His in the city. We might almost say this homeless wanderer has become the man of many homes.

Indeed it was always home where Jesus was. The little room in Capernaum is far away behind Him now; but the love-circle is still unbroken. And where love is there is home. They had left all to follow Him, but Jesus said—and they knew His word was true—"There is no man that hath left home or brethren, or sisters, or

Jesus the Householder

father, or mother, or wife, or children, or lands for my sake ... but he shall receive an hundredfold now in this time ... and in the world to come eternal life." His presence was home to them. For home is not the four walls of a house, but just Love—Love that cherishes, Love that defends and protects, yea, and Love that serves, that spends itself for the beloved even to the uttermost. See them in that upper room in Jerusalem—the last forming of the home-circle round a common board. No servant to wait on them, no humble slave to wash their feet. But the 'Master of the house' Himself rises, girds a towel round His waist, and fulfils that lowly service for them all—including the traitor. And He knew! So the Master of the house takes the place of the lowliest slave of the household. That is the noblest, the one perfect realization in the world's history, of the spirit, the inner secret of the word Home. But more: it is the complete disclosure, before the disciple-circle, of the supreme Law of the Kingdom of Heaven. The greatest is He that serveth; for the Heavenly Father is the most self-effacing servant of creation. 'Greater love hath no man than this,' His disciples were thinking as He

Jesus the Citizen

washed their feet. And to-morrow He was to die—to die for them.

It was the last night of the Master of the house with His family. And He began to tell them that it was so. 'With desire have I desired to eat the Pascal meal with you before I go; for I say unto you I will not any more eat thereof until it be fulfilled in the Kingdom of God. . . . In a little while—in a very little while, ye shall see my face no more. . . . To-morrow the Shepherd will be smitten and the sheep scattered. . . . The silence of deepest sorrow had fallen on them as they listened, and their lips were mute. Perhaps He rose then from the table, and hiding His face from them for a moment, stood there at the open door of that room on the roof of the house, chosen possibly in memory of the little room in Capernaum. There above Him spread " the magic significant night, silent, too, but silent with excess of meaning," crowded with throbbing stars. We think we can see Him stretching His hand out and up towards that sight, as He turned half-round to speak to them. And like soft bars of music that prelude some great symphony—nay, stranger, sweeter far— the great words fell: " Let not your heart be

Jesus the Householder

troubled. Believe in God, yea, believe in me. In my Father's house are many mansions. If it were not so I would have told you. I go to prepare a place for you. . . . I will come again and receive you to myself, that where I am there you may be also. . . ." Still thinking of Home —the eternal Home.

It was all but the last moment in the circle of the earthly home. To-morrow He was to leave them. To-morrow He was to set out on the unknown journey, homeless, homeless, into the pitch black night of death. That Cross is the deepest assurance of the life for ever. In a universe that contains love like that, there is no death. He became homeless that Home might be the last sure reality to men.

VIII

THE HOLY CITY

It has been the distinction of certain cities in the course of the world's history to win a permanent individuality for themselves. Athens, for example, is the shrine of artistic beauty, Rome is the cradle of order and public justice, Babylon is the symbol of sensuality, Paris is the world-type of gaiety, London stands for commerce, trafficking; but Jerusalem is enshrined for ever in the story of the world as the symbol-city of religious faith. It is pre-eminently ' the Holy City.' The Hebrews of the Old Testament dispensation called it by that name. When they came to the land of Palestine they already found it reckoned, among the pre-historic Canaanites, a peculiarly holy place. Its name was ' City of Peace ' (Uru-Salem); and its King was Melchizedek, King of Righteousness, King of the Most High God. When David made it the capital of the Jewish nation, its Temple gradually became the central shrine, the supreme high place, the only

The Holy City

sanctuary where the glory of God came down to dwell with men. In the land of exile they opened their windows towards it, to pray. In the days of Christ, all the roads of the world led to its gates, and were worn by the feet of ceaseless multitudes of pilgrims. In the Middle Ages it was the objective of the Crusades. In those days when the world was thought to be flat, it was reckoned the centre of the world: the round stone is still shown in the so-called sepulchre of Christ, which was supposed to mark the very hub of the cosmic wheel. The Moslem who recently held the city in his devastating rule called it El-Kuds, the Holy City; and it is part of the pathos of the modern Jew—scattered and broken as is the race through all the nations of the earth to-day—that his hour of deepest emotion is when he turns his passionate eyes of longing towards its dear and sacred walls, or when he stands in the place of wailing, beating his head against the foundation stones of the ancient Temple. Christendom can never forget that the Cross was reared on Calvary beside it. Yes, Jerusalem is still the Holy City of the world.

Let us remember also with reverence that for

Jesus the Citizen

our Lord it was the Holy City, too. He shared the patriotic devotion and the expectations of His race which gathered there. It was ever the central scene in all His dreams and longings. It was there He saw, concentrated in one unutterable sigh of sorrow, all humanity's brokenness, and need, and despair. It was there He heard most clearly, above all the din and roar of time, the voice of His heavenly Father, calling Him to service and sacrifice for the redemption of the world.

For we must also remind ourselves that though it was named the Holy City, " the City of Peace," there was no city in all the world " whose soil has been more repeatedly drenched with the blood of its people—the thousands who have perished by the sword, within these grey walls, from the time when 'the children of Judah smote it with the edge of the sword, and set it on fire,' to the day when Geoffrey de Bouillon and his knights rode in a stream of blood reaching to their saddle-girths to recover the Holy Sepulchre." Yes, and we might add, until the day when Allenby walked into the liberated city, when it fell in the Great European War. During the five thousand three hundred

The Holy City

years of its existence, it had only 500 years of real independence. It sustained more than twenty sieges: twice it was sacked and razed to the ground—once, when the Babylonians came in 586 B.C. and carried the nation into exile, and again, in A.D. 70, when the Roman Titus left not one stone standing on another, as our Lord Himself predicted. The prey of Persian, Macedonian, Syrian, Egyptian, Greek, Roman, the Crusader and Islam in turn, it was ever the scene of inward strife and faction as well. "The picture of Jerusalem and its people," says Sir Walter Besant, "during the fifty years which preceded the destruction of the city by Titus is nowhere surpassed in all the dark annals of religious zeal." We do not sufficiently realize this when we are thinking of our Lord's career. Jesus was born "amid the fever of the establishment of the Roman power in Judæa."

Let us recall in barest outline some of the terrible happenings in Jerusalem about the time of Christ. When He was born the career of Herod the Great was drawing to its stormy close—clouds of rebellion hanging over an angry blood-red sunset. When, in fulsome flattery of Rome, his protectress, Herod reared

Jesus the Citizen

a golden eagle over the gate of the Temple, and the riotous mob tore it to the ground and publicly destroyed it, Herod in revenge made a living bonfire of forty of the ringleaders, and others were executed in less terrible ways. The massacre of the innocents round Bethlehem and Jerusalem is told in the sacred narrative, and is quite in keeping with the character of the man. When the hour of his death drew near, he shut in the Hippodrome the most illustrious of the Jews, with orders that they should be executed when he died, so that the city might be filled with mourning, even if not for him.

At the very next Passover, after the accession of Archelaus, his heir, the deep-stirred feelings of the crowd found vent in a riot, in which three thousand Jews were massacred. Seven weeks later they rose in a rebellion which Varus, the Roman Proconsul of Syria, had to come with an army from Antioch to quell. As a climax to his work of ruthless suppression, he crucified two thousand Jews.

Ten years later there was a faction fight between Jews and Samaritans who had defiled the Temple by flinging some dead bodies into its cloisters. It was about this time too that the

The Holy City

first rebellion of the Zealots took place. There followed a long twelve or thirteen years marked by plotting and scheming, in which Pharisees strove with Sadducees for possession of the High Priesthood and the lucrative offices of the Temple.

Then came Pilate, intending to make a great show of authority. He introduced Cæsar's effigy into the city, only to be startled and puzzled by the fanaticism of the crowd which came clamouring for its removal. They refused to be dispersed, bared their necks, and bade his soldiers come on. And Pilate had to give way. Later, he built a great aqueduct to the city. But he pillaged the Temple treasury to pay for the work; and the crowd again rose with angry outcries. This time a massacre ensued. And it is probably this that is referred to when Jesus was told of the " Galileans whose blood Pilate had mingled with their sacrifices." Need we wonder that in this excitable, unstable city, seething with faction and rebellion, Christ, according to the Fourth Gospel, should twice have been threatened with stoning? There already all the conditions were present that made the Cross.

Jesus the Citizen

With what mingled emotions this city, so sacred yet so drenched with blood, must have filled the spirit of Jesus! It was the city of His childhood's fancies. He had heard its ancient story at His mother's knee. He had listened to the pilgrims' glowing descriptions of the glory of its great Temple now restored. Many a time He must have wistfully watched the road that led to it through the Samarian hills as He stood on the height behind Nazareth. And who can doubt that the holy light of His Father's smile broke through the last dim questioning wonderment of His soul when He stood at length within the Temple gates? Under the Pascal moon and the glittering stars of those two nights of ecstasy when He tarried behind in Jerusalem, all fear and loneliness for ever banished from His soul, we can see Him standing, the word of a Psalm breaking in whispered rapture from His lips: " When I consider the heavens, the work of Thy fingers, the moon and the stars which Thou hast ordained, what is man that Thou art mindful of him, or the son of man that Thou visitest him?" . . . 'And yet Thou hast visited me—this son of man—my Father!' Yes, it was surely in Jerusalem that this sense

The Holy City

of the Presence of God broke with overwhelming force on the young boy's soul.

Yet He must have gone back from Jerusalem with a sadness in His heart, though scarcely knowing why. To some degree He must have been made aware of the city's restlessness, must have heard the uneasy whisperings and angry mutterings, and must have seen about the Temple courts the so-called priests of God behave like grasping merchantmen. And He must have vaguely felt that there was something wrong. Year after year this faithful pilgrim went to the feasts, and may even sometimes have witnessed a tumult on the city streets. Year after year this sadness deepened in His heart, deepened into the sorrow of a great pity, deepened into the anger and the agony of love, deepened into burning tears of longing and of vicarious shame.

We are sometimes told that Jesus was the Prophet of Galilee, who preached a bright and sunny gospel among the hills and by the Lake to the common people, whom He knew so well. And the question is asked, Why did He ever make up His mind to leave it? What compulsion was there that drove Him from the circle of His native hills to face the rude, alien stare of this

Jesus the Citizen

haughty city, which despised His land, laughed at His accent, and cursed His countrymen for their disobedience to the Law? Why did He not stay and continue His Gospel of joy among the hills? The great crowds followed Him there. Some were disillusioned, it is true; but multitudes laughed and wept in the sunshine of His radiant presence, casting for ever behind them the winter of their despair. What possessed Him to leave it all, and set His face towards Jerusalem? And this answer to these questions is sometimes given, that this popularity turned His head.

When He began, these pedants say, He had no thought of posing as Messiah. But gradually the growing consciousness of His power, and the foolish flattery of His admirers, instilled it into His mind that He must be the chosen One of God. And if He was the Messiah, then He must appear in the Holy City and make good His claim. He Himself believed at first, they tell us, that God would establish the kingdom of heaven upon earth through Him. And when the gathering clouds of opposition began to darken His hopes, He nevertheless persisted in His strange infatuation, and deliberately courted

The Holy City

death, believing that God would immediately raise Him up again to complete the work He had begun. "Can it be," asks Mrs. Humphrey Ward, one of the most literary of these modern doubters, "that even the pain of fond illusions shattered also entered into the Passion of the Son of Man?"

What shall we answer to this strange reading of the life of Love? Can it be that the pain of being misunderstood is still one of the swords that pierce through the soul of the Son of Man? Why should we seek to be continually refashioning the Christ according to the pattern of our pedantic theories instead of letting the facts speak for themselves? But to the modern doctrinaire Christ will ever be just a doctrinaire, a man carried away by foolish fads and notions. Was it a mere theory about Messiahship that was the governing impetus of this great Life? Was it a mind obsessed with a dogma of the schools? Was it—forgive the irreverence of putting into plain words the insinuation of these critics of the Lord—was it conceit inflated by popular flattery that filled this noble mind with a hallucination bordering on insanity? Oh, blindness of the human heart!

Jesus the Citizen

Not doctrinairianism or conceit, but love was the motive power that ruled every action of this life from first to last—love turned to burning pain at the sight of His people's wrongs, love wrung with anguish at the touch of sin. It was love that made Him stoop to be baptized in Jordan—love gazing on the crowds assembled as He had never before seen them assembled, in misery of outward and inward want, listening with a yearning wonder to the Baptist's message, and with a murmur like a sigh unsatisfied. It was love that drew Him down from the quiet hills of Nazareth to the teeming, restless life of the cities by the Lake. It was love that made Him turn on the alien shores of Tyre, and sigh His soul towards His native land and His people, the lost sheep of the House of Israel. It was love that led Him to a renewed consecration on the slopes of Hermon, where every reason that prudence or ambition could allege was promptly answered by the dictates of His heart's compassion. Even death must not deter Him from obeying the call of love. Yes, it was love that drove Him from the circle of the Galilean hills into the blaze of Jerusalem's publicity. That last journey from Galilee to Jerusalem was the most heroic pil-

The Holy City

grimage ever undertaken by the beautiful feet of love. He knew the things that belonged to that distracted city's peace. Could He lay the burden on His soul of refusing to tell her—of failing to make one last grand effort to show His people—the whole lost race of Israel—the way back to God? And when He reached at length the Temple Courts and began His last campaign, once more He had that strange and blessed experience which visited Him at the baptism and in the hour of holy resolve on Hermon, when a whisper, as if from the overarching skies, stole into His soul, and He knew that obeying the impulse of love He had won the approval of God.

Strange words were on His lips at times, words which seem at first sight to justify the theories of the pedants: " It cannot be that a prophet perish out of Jerusalem." But let us remember the occasion on which these words were spoken. They are the only words of sarcastic contempt that ever fell from our Lord's lips, so far as the records show. They were spoken in answer to the guile of a craven-hearted king. Jesus' presence was making the wretched monarch uncomfortable, for he thought the

Jesus the Citizen

Master was the ghost of John the Baptist risen from the dead; and he wanted Him put out of the way. It was in answer to this desire that Jesus spoke the words, "It cannot be that a prophet perish out of Jerusalem." Probably also Jesus involved the Pharisees, who bore the message, in the same sarcastic condemnation, when He spoke His reply. There is grim irony here; it shows that His resolve was already taken to go to Jerusalem. And when He saw those Pharisees before Him, He thought of the people who slew the prophets there. He knew too well what He had to face in the Holy City. It was blind pride. That is why the broad impression of all our Lord's labours in Jerusalem seems to be that the sunny gospel is lost in a tangle of disputings and angry denunciations.

His words of love could make no impression on a mask of hypocrisy and supercilious disdain. And His holy heart could only speak against the awful sham in the language of revolt—angry revolt, which slowly lifted itself into one last passionate, overwhelming cry of love: "O Jerusalem, Jerusalem, that killest the prophets, and stonest them which are sent unto thee, how often would I have gathered thy children together

The Holy City

even as a hen gathereth her chickens under her wings, and ye would not ! Behold, your house is left unto you desolate. For I say unto you, ye shall not see me henceforth, till ye shall say, Blessed is He that cometh in the name of the Lord."

It is always the cities that have destroyed the prophets. Jerusalem is named the Holy City, but we think of it as such, not because of the arrogant ecclesiastical bureaucracy which fancied itself the guardian of its holiness. They builded the tombs of the prophets, and garnished the sepulchres of the righteous, and marvelled at the shocking shortsightedness of their fathers that had stoned them—all unconscious that theirs was the very temper that had slain the prophets—all unconscious that standing in their midst was One that was greater than all the prophets, One whom their scornful pride, turned to malicious spite, was in a few brief days to impale upon a Roman gallows-beam.

Cities have short memories. The pierced Feet still come and go along the streets of the cities of to-day; and they are still treated with the old familiar scorn. Blind pride is still the cross on which the Lord is crucified afresh. Looking

Jesus the Citizen

back across those 1900 years we speak of those Pharisees in the very way in which they spoke of their fathers: "If we had been in Jerusalem in the days of those Pharisees we would not have crucified Jesus of Nazareth. We honour His memory to-day. We have all of us, even the high priests of modern progress, gone the length of putting Jesus into the niche of immortality as one of the world's master-forces. We are all very busy building His tomb—yes, His tomb. We seem to think that it was just one or two great ideas that this Master-soul came to set moving, in the world of time. We are always using those ideas—proudly, as if we had made them our own. And up in this world of ideas we have forgotten all about the real facts of the case—forgotten that men toil and struggle and blunder, and come to grief, and soil their souls hopelessly, and perish; and that it was a new power He came to impart to men, to lift them from the morass.

We are committing a dreadful error if we think it is honour—what the world calls fame—Christ wants. That was not what brought Him to Jerusalem. He does not want us to build His tomb, to garnish His sepulcre. It is not myrrh and cassia and aloes—the embalming of a glorious

The Holy City

memory—He wants. He has put death and the grave for ever behind Him. It is the living Christ, the Christ who stands in our midst to-day, with whom we have to do. He is what He does, and He redeems from sin. When we open our hearts in a great confession that we need redemption His crucifixion becomes one more triumph, a real and present triumph, and not merely an antique spectacle, glorified in history.

IX

THE BLIND CITY

STAND on the western slopes of the Mount of Olives, overlooking the deep gorge of the Kidron, and dream yourself back to the hour when from that same hill-side, One looked with weeping eyes and cried, " If thou hadst known, even thou, at least in this thy day, the things which belong unto thy peace ! " . . . You look across to the west, and you see the high ridge of Judea, the backbone of Palestine slipping down to a sharp tongue of rock which shoots out between the valley of Hinnom on the further side of the city and Kidron's deep ravine, which cuts across the foreground of the scene. There on that tongue of rock the Holy City huddles, mass behind mass, a petrified avalanche just caught as it seems on the very edge of the cliffs ere it had precipitated itself into the gorges. At the sharp angle where the two valleys meet the city seems not only to have been arrested in its descent

The Blind City

into the gorge, but to have shrunk back somewhat in shuddering recoil. Not far away from that gloomy meeting-place of valleys is the field of blood, where Judas went and hanged himself. The city itself has the appearance of an immense fortress. Historians have often recalled together these two weeping figures, Titus who " gazed upon Jerusalem from Scopus the day before its destruction, and wept for the sake of the beautiful city, and Jesus Christ who when things were ripening for Titus foresaw the coming of the legions, as He looked upon Jerusalem from Olivet, and when He was come near He beheld the city and wept over it." " If thou hadst known—if thou hadst known ... but now they are hid from thine eyes." Before many years the words of an ancient lament might have been written again as its epitaph: "How is the gold become dim! How is the most fine gold changed! The stones of the sanctuary are poured out in the top of every street."

There is the waving line of the city wall running along the edge of that steep bank above the Kidron. Immediately behind it, crowding to the very edge of the ravine and rising from it

Jesus the Citizen

like a glittering exhalation are the courts and colonnades of the great Temple, restored by Herod to a greater glory than even Solomon had devised. Behind that, a lofty bridge spans the Tyropœan depression which runs north and south through the heart of the city. Behind that again, climbing westward up the slopes, rise the city's splendid towers and stately edifices, its council-chambers, its hippodrome, its amphitheatre; and, crowning the horizon, Herod's strong palace, its gardens grimly fortified with towers. The Temple courts are thronged with pilgrims from all parts of the world; its high altar, the rock Moriah, smokes with ceaseless sacrifice. Floating across the valley comes the chanting of the priests, singing their Hallels, and the subdued roar and rustle of the moving throng, the tumult of a living sea.

There in those Temple Courts, a few weeks since, according to the Fourth Gospel, the Prophet of Galilee stood and moved the crowds to wonder with His words; and the haughty priests and scribes and Pharisees to angry threats of death. There in the lingering autumn, on the last day of the Feast of Tabernacles, when

The Blind City

the priests in stately procession were bearing up the water in golden vessels from the pool of Siloam, singing the ancient hymn: " With joy shall ye draw water from the well of salvation," that Galilean Peasant, whose face was like a king's in its majesty, stood out before the watching throng and cried: " If any man thirst let him come to me and drink." There on that same day when evening fell, and the golden candelabra in the Court of the Women were lighted, and the worshippers danced before them with blazing torches in their hands, He stood again and cried, saying: " I am the Light of the world: he that followeth me shall not walk in the darkness, but will have the light of life."

There when the feast was over and the pilgrims were gone, He reasoned day after day with the rulers and the inhabitants of the Holy City, until, driven to distraction by their hardness of heart, He cried, " Oh, wherefore do I speak to you at all ? When ye have lifted up the Son of man, then shall ye recognize that I am He, and of Myself do nothing, but, as the Father taught Me, speak these things." And those children of the seed of Abraham would have stoned Him for blasphemy, but He slipped from them and was

Jesus the Citizen

gone. There, too, when He saw the blind beggar, whom He healed, excommunicated from Jewish privileges and pronounced as dead, because of his courageous testimony, He called him and all the wandering multitude to another fold with that word of tender comfort: " I am the true Shepherd ... my sheep hear my voice ... and other sheep I have which are not of this fold. Them also must I lead, and to my voice they shall hearken; and there shall be one flock, one shepherd. . . . I will lay down my life for the sheep."

There, finally, in the wintry December, at the Feast of Dedication, while He still clung wistfully to the place, seeking to win the city for His Father, He found Himself at last ringed round by the maddened rulers, crying, " How long dost thou keep us in suspense ? If thou art Messiah, tell us plainly." And He answered, " I and my Father are one." And if it had not been for the protection of the friendly pilgrim crowd with which the city streets were once more thronged, He would most certainly this time have been pelted to death by the infuriated priests and their sycophants. But He passed through the crowded streets unscathed, and left the city to

The Blind City

return no more until He came to die. It was then probably that He uttered this lament: "O Jerusalem, Jerusalem, thou that killest the prophets and stonest them which are sent unto thee, how often would I have gathered thy children together, even as a hen gathereth her chickens under her wings, and ye would not! Behold your house is left unto you desolate. For I say unto you, Ye shall not see me henceforth, till ye shall say Blessed is He that cometh in the name of the Lord."

That was but a few short weeks ago. And now the spring has come. All the vegetation of the hill-side is bursting into fair, green life again. Once more the mighty crowds have gathered from all quarters to this holy spot. It is the eve of the great Pascal Feast. Once again the distant roar of the busy streets comes floating across the valley. Could we transport ourselves for a moment to these busy streets we should hear strange words, excited words: 'Has He come? Is He coming? Will He come?' Who is this who seems to be occupying all their thoughts, driving out all thoughts of festival? Down in Gethsemane the cedars have already hushed their restless boughs, and

Jesus the Citizen

stand a solemn congregation awaiting the dread scene shortly to be enacted there. Along the road that bends around the hill from Bethany the flocks of little Pascal lambs are bleating pitifully, as they come slowly toward the city of doom.

> All in the April morning,
> April airs were abroad;
> The sheep with their little lambs
> Pass'd me by on the road
>
> The lambs were weary, and crying
> With a weak human cry;
> I thought on the Lamb of God
> Going meekly to die.

And by the roadside groups of pilgrims are waiting, straining eager looks along that same road. And see, a crowd comes into view shouting, cheering, singing, waving palm branches, casting them down before a solitary figure on an ass: ' Hozannah to the Son of David ! Blessed is He that cometh in the name of the Lord ! Hozannah in the highest ! ' Onward He comes, meek and lowly and riding upon an ass. Is He mad ? Have the plaudits of the multitude turned His head ? Does He think now to move that hardened city ? Humble and weaponless

The Blind City

with His unarmed bodyguard, will He drive the Roman usurper out? Ah, He comes to where we stand. He gently stays the ass. And turning round in full view of the city, He gazes out across the valley, and the tears break from His eyes. And, as the hush of awe passes over that rejoicing throng, there comes from His lips the cry: " If thou hadst known . . . if thou hadst known the things that belong to thy peace ! But now . . . but now . . . they are hid from thine eyes." No, He is not deluded. He knows. Too well He knows.

> " Ride on, ride on in majesty,
> In lowly pomp ride on—to die."

Deep was the significance of these tears in the subsequent course of history. For one hour He had permitted all the vain, deluded hopes of the popular excitement to gather about Him, as they called Him King in open defiance of the Roman power. Then came that dramatic pause, and then the burst of patriot tears. It seemed to the crowd as though an icy wind had swept through the generous sunlight of the hour. And when they reached the streets, in chill discouragement, they could only answer the

Jesus the Citizen

scornful, 'Who is this?' of the by-standers by saying tamely it was the Prophet of Nazareth of Galilee. And in the Temple courts at length, only shrill piping children's voices, all innocent of harm, cried, "Blessed is the King who comes in the name of the Lord!" Those tears quenched for ever the last effort of popular patriotic folly. Those tears meant that the nation was taking her own way of devising political rebellion; He had in view a movement that transcended all earthly politics. Disappointment speedily became resentment. Their great hero had turned out a fool, they thought. He had deluded them, made them a laughing-stock, betrayed them. Resentment speedily fermented into a lust for revenge. In a few days they were clamouring, 'Crucify Him! Crucify Him!'

What sort of Christ is it that our respectable modern city is prepared to welcome? A Christ who will free us from the incubus of social obligation, so that we will no longer have to pay our rates in sorrow and our taxes in anger—a Christ who will smash the tyranny of an effete social order—a Christ who will march at the head of our country's legions to victory, unconcerned whether the conscience of the nation has been

The Blind City

brought to repentance? Oh, we may do our best to spread for Him our palm-branches of theory and our garments of organization, and to welcome Him with shouting. But verily He will stay the procession to weep, and weep again. We are beginning at the wrong end. We will not take the trouble to recognize the things that belong to our peace. The mind of the city is notoriously short-sighted. One day it shouts ' Hail, King ! ' and the next, light-heartedly, ' His blood be upon our heads.' Out of the midst of modern democracy the hungry sheep look up and are not fed because they have turned away from the true Shepherd, and will not hear His voice.

" What have I heard on the streets of my city?
What have I seen where the hill-paths wind?
Multitudes, multitudes scattered abroad:
Pauper imploring pauper for pity,
Blind men clutching the skirts of the blind,
Multitudes waiting a Shepherd from God!

Scattered abroad like sheep on the mountains,
Shepherdless, waiting in vain to be fed,
Harassed and burdened, sick with neglect,
Never at morning led forth to the fountains,
Never at eve to the pastures led,
How should they know Him, whom now they reject?

Jesus the Citizen

How should ye know your Shepherd was tender?
Lantern, nor sheep-call, nor staff have ye known:
Full are the mouths of your prophets with lying:
Oh, my people, my people, the splendour
Of Israel dawns not from Temple or throne:
But I have a dream of a Shepherd . . .dying. . . . "[1]

For, think once again of those tears, such tears falling from such eyes. Do they not seem to speak a message of Divine Defeat? The Son of God wept on Olivet because He saw the shadows rushing down to obliterate Jerusalem's day of grace. Here is a solemn mystery of Time, indeed. All the pity of God cannot avail to avert the inevitable wheels of the judgment car of History. That would be to undo the bands of His own holiness. Nothing in heaven or earth can avail to defeat the Divine Holiness. But the Divine Pity may be defeated —by defiant human pride. There is one sight in Jerusalem to-day which might well move the traveller to tears. It is the double-arched gate Beautiful, forth from which the scapegoat used to issue, bearing the people's sins to the wilderness, and through which, according to ancient tradition, the Messiah was to enter the city on

[1] *Poems Second Book*, by Edith Anne Stewart

The Blind City

His return. That gate is now built up with solid masonry, "affording neither entrance for Christ nor exit for sin." It is a symbol of the city's fate.

But were those Divine tears tears of resentment, tears of chagrin, tears of despair? Nay, they were tears only of yearning compassion and unutterable love. Strange paradox! Defeated and crucified compassion is the one thing that will conquer the world some day. The Cross can never be defeated. The symbol of Defeat has become the Symbol of Victory. Bending over every city of the modern world, where the message of the Cross has come, the Christ of God still weeps in glory. The gate Beautiful in any modern city may or may not be built to the very keystone with the mortar of human pride. But every heart has its own Zion, and its own day of grace which it may reject. To every heart there may come a voice through the gathering gloom, the voice of One who weeps because of love despised: "If *thou* hadst known, even thou, at least in this thy day, the things that belong to thy peace! But now they are hid from thine eyes."

X

THE CITY OF THE CROSS

It is with minds subdued and solemnized that we would seek to pass back once again across the centuries to old Jerusalem, to view from a certain aspect the scene on the page of time which most haunts the world with horror and with glory. It is not on the Mount of Olives that we stand now, though that was an imposing scene as we gazed across the valley to the West at the great mass of the city's masonry poised upon that shelving angle of rocky hill. Nor is it a story of tears in the midst of apparent triumph that we now contemplate: it is a spectacle of immortal courage in the midst of defeat and ignominy and shame.

Let us approach the city by the great North road that leads from Galilee and beyond it, through Samaria, to its sacred gates. Here there is no deep valley, but a flat, uninteresting approach, rolling slowly down from the high Judæan watershed. This was the city's vul-

The City of the Cross

nerable side. This was ever the objective of the attacking foe. Across this side, left by nature thus defenceless, King Hezekiah built the city's strongest wall, high, massive, and frowning, fortified by many splendid towers. The gate that pierces the wall ahead of us is the Damascus Gate. We can see practically nothing of the city itself as we approach, nothing but that black, forbidding wall shutting in all the city's holy pride and respectability, shutting out a dreary and untidy scene. Fitting symbol is that wall, of the city's prejudice and exclusiveness and selfish hate that shut the Saviour out at last to a vulgar death—" despised and rejected of men."

Here on the left as we pass on toward the Gate is a somewhat sombre spot, the ancient burying-place of Kings. There on the right is a great, dark, barren cinder-heap, the ashes of centuries of Temple sacrifice: a pathetic sight.

> " Not all the blood of beasts
>   On Jewish altars slain
>   Can give the guilty conscience peace,
>   Or wash away the stain."

Further in on the other side of the road lies an ugly quarry hole, where Herod's workmen are

Jesus the Citizen

still hewing stones for the now almost completed and very gorgeous restoration of the Temple. Then close by and just beyond it to the left there rises a green mound, having at one end a precipitous limestone rock, protruding like the jaw-bone of some giant's skull. The ignorant felaheen still call it the place of stoning, though felons are no more brought here to die. And it is said that the Jew when he passes it still breathes to himself the strange words, " Cursed be he who destroyed our nation by aspiring to be its king." Mark well the spot. It was once called Golgotha, ' the knoll of the skull.' Lone and bare it stands to-day. Not many years since, it was, as we are fain to believe, rightly identified. Who that stands there—kneels there, perhaps, in prayer too deep for words—can help being grateful to God that the tradition which placed the site of the Holy Sepulchre in the heart of the city was almost certainly mistaken ? For there the Eastern Churches have built their shrines, and now crowd and jostle each other, in unseemly rivalry, while here the open sky looks down upon the bare, green mound.

We pass within the shadow of the wall's grim towers, and enter the gate about six or seven in

The City of the Cross

the early morning of Friday the 7th April in the year A.D. 29. To-morrow is the greatest Sabbath of the Jewish year, the Feast of Passover. To-day is the day of holy preparation. Crowds of pilgrims are already on the streets: they have come in for morning sacrifice. There is an appearance of mingled solemnity and restlessness about the crowd. Something unusual is afoot to-day. The hush of the approaching ceremonial is upon them. Priests flit through the throng; the Pharisees make a special display of phylacteries; the elders and scribes wear an extra-grave demeanour, as if it devolved on them to sustain the dignity of the occasion. But we pass along David Street, and we notice that there is much subdued and eager discussion going on among the crowd. Some are shaking solemn heads, some muttering curses, some are dumb and bewildered. And here and there we catch an ill-suppressed sneer of wicked joy. What are the people saying? There are rumours of a dark and sinister deed the night before. The Prophet of Nazareth was treacherously surprised among the cedars of Gethsemane. And there are confused reports of an ugly and shameful scene in the mansion house on the slopes of the Mount

Jesus the Citizen

of Olives, where dwelt Annas, an aged worldling and the ex-High Priest. And early this morning —yes, for some of the crowd witnessed the incident—the Reformer of Galilee was hustled rapidly and furtively into the city, pale-faced, bright-eyed for want of sleep, up through the Temple precincts to the Hall of Hewn Stone, where the Sanhedrin met to deliberate and to judge.

What did it all mean? What was this Sanhedrin? Composed of priests and Pharisees and elders, it was the Town Council of Jerusalem, it was the Parliament of the Jewish people, it was the highest judicial tribunal, the last court of appeal in the land; and it was also the supreme court of the Jewish Church. For the Mosaic Law, the Law of God, the sacred document of the people's faith, was also the common law of the land. True, the Romans had conquered Palestine: Pilate's Prætorium was only a stone's throw away. But the Romans in their remarkable practical wisdom seldom disturbed a conquered people's laws. They left the Jews their Sanhedrin with all its powers intact, except the supreme right, the right of dispensing death in cases of capital offence. That was annoying, for they were bent on death to-day.

The City of the Cross

A highly respectable body, this, met to deal out justice. Justice to these rulers consisted in maintaining those laws, built to conserve worn-out institutions which had long since become a heavy burden and a fraud and sham. The noble aspirations and dreams of great reformers were outside its scope. Justice to them was a case of preserving the great fabric of social respectability. And here was the Galilean Peasant whom they had long sought to entrap, at length in their clutches. It would hardly do to ask how. That would not be very respectful. The trial, if there was a trial, was apparently already over. Begun, continued and ended in the course of a single night, it was very irregular. But a meeting of the court to-day at day-break to confirm the verdict would make it all formally correct, legal, and respectable. So the formal trial began with the hearing of witnesses *against* the accused. That was a violation of the Mosaic procedure, which ordained that witnesses for the defence should always be examined first. Moreover, those witnesses had been sought for by the judges. That was a most unusual performance. Their evidence did not square, unfortunately. The judge had to take to cross-questioning the

Jesus the Citizen

Prisoner, though the Hebrew law refused to sanction that. Then he angrily demanded a confession, though their learned lawyers had said that that was wrong.

But what could he do with a prisoner who never broke the silence to answer a single question? That majestic silence flurried and flustered them into ever wilder irregularities of procedure, till at last they passed sentence of guilt on a charge of blasphemy, though Jesus had only claimed to be that for which all Israel looked with hope and expectation. Moreover, they passed sentence twenty-four hours before it was legal so to do. Was it not unseemly haste? Ah, well, they had to deal with a dangerous innovator, who was defying the conventions, and they must take Him when they had Him. If they waited twenty-four hours they would have to postpone the condemnation until after the feast. It would not be respectable to have a man tried and hanged on Holy Day. And if they waited the people might have recovered from their stupor of surprise—this people who knew not the law and were accursed. The fact is they had not met to try the offender. They had met to find a pretext for destroying one whom

The City of the Cross

they had already in their hearts condemned. It was all done in the interests of respectability. And surely respectability covers a multitude of illegalities, irregularities and shameful wrongs.

For He *was* a dangerous man. For months, up and down the land, He had been setting all the people against their betters, making them discontented with the existing social order. And had He not shamefully broken their holy Sabbath? Had He not challenged their ecclesiastical authority? Had He not spoken disrespectfully of the sacred Law of Moses? Had he not spoken of the day when His Gospel would end the Temple worship, sanctified since the days of Solomon by centuries of sacrifice? Nay, had He not denounced their vested interests that day, when He cleared the Temple courts of trafficking? What would become of the great fabric of respectability, if this sort of thing were allowed to go on? Surely it was excusable to stretch a legal point or two, when respectability so clamantly demanded it.

But if they had already condemned Jesus, why this mockery of a trial at all? Well, it was death they wanted, and there was Pilate to face. That was the annoying thing. They had to find

Jesus the Citizen

a pretext to make to Pilate. And that is the stage we find them at, as we now enter the prætorian courtyard along with the crowd. Will He get justice there at the hands of the Procurator from Rome—Rome the great fountain of all the principles from which modern jurisprudence springs? Will He get it from this brusque, practical man, with his supreme contempt for all things Jewish? It is hardly likely; for here we have merely a selfish, cynical, craven-hearted materialist, anxious to preserve his Roman dignity in the face of these slaves of Rome.

"What is your charge?" he asks with haughty insolence.

"Charge?" they answer with sullen defiance to the man they had three times already cowed. "We have not brought Him here to accuse Him. We have already tried Him and found Him guilty."

"If you are so jealous of your law," Pilate angrily retorts, "take Him, and deal with Him accordingly."

"We may not put Him to death," was their grudging but significant reply.

"Death!" thinks the sobered governor. Then it was a capital offence. "What is the crime?" he asks.

The City of the Cross

And those priests who had condemned Jesus for the religious offence of calling Himself Messiah twisted their sentence into a lie. " He has been calling Himself a King, and setting Himself up against Cæsar."

Turning to the meek and solitary figure, pale, dishevelled, roped, silent, Pilate asked in tones of pity, contempt and wonder, " Art thou a King ? "

" My Kingdom," said the Man, looking at the Roman with His haunting eyes, " My Kingdom is not of this world."

Something gripped the heart of Pilate. What ? Another dreamer, another of their mad Messiahs ? And yet—so different from the rest. ' Not of this world ? ' It is strange ! Turning back to the mob, he said, with trouble in his voice: " I find no fault in Him."

He was in an awkward dilemma. The Prisoner was clearly innocent, yet this mob was as clearly intent upon His death. What could it mean ? Listening to the hubbub the Procurator caught the word ' Galilee.' " Galilee ! ah, that is Herod's jurisdiction. And Herod is in town. I shall send Him there." But this ruse, born of his eagerness to shuffle off responsibility, com-

Jesus the Citizen

pletely failed. Not one word could Herod draw from Jesus. And so, joining in the ribald mockery of his men-at-arms, he sent Him back to Pilate.

Then Pilate tried a second ruse. It was the rulers who were clamouring for Jesus' death. If He were a popular reformer, perhaps the people were on His side. Let them be put to the test. " This is the season of your Feast," he said, " when it is the custom to release a criminal to you. Shall I release this Jesus ? "

But as he paused to listen to a messenger with a tale of warning from his wife, those priests, turning to the gathered crowd, urged them not to become the tool of this haughty Roman. " Ask for Jesus," they said, " but not this Jesus—Jesus Barabbas." And when Pilate was listening again, they were howling, " Not this man, but Barabbas."

" Then what shall I do with Jesus, the Messiah ? " asked the disconcerted Governor.

And they shouted back, " Let Him be crucified."

" Why, what evil has He done ? "

" Let Him be crucified ! Crucify Him ! Crucify Him ! "

The City of the Cross

Then it was that amid the growing tumult Pilate sent for his sorry, little basin of water. Many a man since has sought to wash his hands in Pilate's basin of weak neutrality. But he only soils the water, and does not cleanse his hands. Carefully Pilate washed his hands. What mattered it a Jew more or less? Perhaps if he thus dramatically thrust responsibility on the people, they would be less eager for Jesus' death.

"His blood be on us and on our children," howled the mob, as they watched his action. Those priests standing in the outer court, lest they should defile themselves in an unclean Gentile's house, could pollute their souls with blood, though they would not pollute their bodies by a breach of ceremonial etiquette.

Then Pilate tried still another plan. He ordered the lictors to scourge Jesus. And the whip with several thongs, each loaded with its ball of lead, curled about the quivering flesh, and cut and tore until the body ran with blood. The soldiers clad the blood-stained figure with the purple military toga; platted a crown of thorns and put it on His head, and set a reed in His hand. Mocking, they knelt and cried, "Hail, King of the Jews." They spat in His

Jesus the Citizen

face, struck Him, and plucking the reed from his hand, smote the thorns into His brow. Then when the sport had gone far enough, Pilate led Him out, a spectacle to move the stones to pity. "Behold the Man!" he cried.

But like wild beasts lusting at the sight of blood, the priests cried, "Crucify! Crucify!"

"Take Him and crucify Him yourselves," shouted the enraged and baffled Pilate.

"Nay, but thou must crucify Him. Thou hast the power. We have the law; and by our law He ought to die, because He made Himself the Son of God."

Son of a god, thought the perplexed and troubled Governor, as once more he approached the strange, disturbing presence. "Whence art Thou, then?" he asked.

It was at this point the bleeding victim spoke a word of pity to the coward wretch. Deeply moved, Pilate told the crowd again that he must release the prisoner.

"If thou release this fellow, thou art not Cæsar's friend. Everyone that maketh himself a King hath insulted Cæsar."

Then Pilate flinched and trembled, but still he hesitated.

The City of the Cross

"Away with Him! Away with Him! Crucify Him," rose the wolfish clamour once again.

"Shall I crucify your King?"

"We have no king but Cæsar," came the swift and ominous retort.

Pilate was beaten. So the tragic drama ended. The laws of pious respectability were maintained. Plainly it was not the grosser sins of the city that reared the Cross; only the sins of the city's conventionality—pride and prejudice. There beneath that sanctimonious cloak there glints the baleful fire of the lowest ring of hell.

And they thrust Him out, beyond that grim North wall, out of that holy city that He should no more pollute the place. And, as they battered the nails through His hands and feet, and lifted Him up on the gruesome knoll, and dropped the Cross into the place prepared for it, His lips moved, and they heard Him say, "Father, forgive them, for they know not what they do."

What was it that happened there, without the city wall? Uncouth, ungainly, vulgar thing—the Cross now stands for a new Law, a new Power, thrusting itself into human life never, nevermore to be pulled down. The new Law, lifted up by immortal courage, beneath the

Jesus the Citizen

darkened heavens, outside the city gate, disconcerting, revolutionary, overturning old forms, defying dead conventions, laying bare the meanness of the shams behind the cloak of respectability, was the Law of Love and Sacrifice. Love that dared to resist the dead hand of custom, love that faced the rude jeers of slow-moving public opinion, love that lifted up its voice against vested interests, love that would stoop down through any shame to claim the souls of men for God.

Is the Cross still outside the city gates in this modern world of ours? Modern society still seeks to hide its social injustices and its shameful anomalies behind the same old cloak of respectability. But the Cross has come into the midst of the city. It is here. It will not be left outside. The Cross has invaded our civic life like a haunting conscience, and will not leave it at rest. Some day it will destroy the last civic and national and social shame. The Law of Respectability which says 'Peace, peace!' when there is no peace is beginning to be driven out by the Law of Love, that hopes and bears, believes, endures, and seeks not its own. For still Christ cries from His Cross to the cities and hearts of men:

The City of the Cross

" A new commandment I give unto you, that ye love one another—not as you love your friends, not as you love yourself, not as you love your Saviour, for that love is a feeble thing, but as I, your Saviour, have loved you."

XI

JESUS AND THE CITY OF GOD

It is a striking fact that, so far as His recorded words permit us to judge, Jesus never visualized the Kingdom of God under the figure of a city. The figure is by no means wanting in the New Testament, but apparently it does not go back to Jesus as its source. It is true we have the vignette parable of the city set on an hill which cannot be hid. And, there Jesus is thinking of the life of the Christian community as a life that is to be conspicuous in its bold protectiveness. But this is practically the only recorded place, except one Oxyrhynchus saying, where He comes near to describing the Kingdom of Heaven under the figure of a city. We cannot help feeling that Jesus fought shy of the conception.

Yet it is no mean figure for the Kingdom. The familiar proverb already referred to on these pages, that God made the country but man made the town is one of those half-truths that in certain relationships become falsehoods. It suggests

Jesus and the City of God

that the conception of the city is something alien to the mind of God. But if God made the country God also made man—made him in His own image. And God made the soul of man a city, a teeming populace of associated thoughts, resolves, imaginings, hopes and fears. That is doubtless the reason why, when man seeks to express himself outwardly in his environment, creating a macrocosm as the reflection of this inner microcosm, he builds cities. For, like the mind of man, a city is the meeting-place of many roads and thoroughfares, a net-work of streets and lanes and traffic-ways where the human herd unites in endless ways to fulfil a common life. Doubtless also, like the soul of man, the city is a place of strange solitudes amid the bustle and clamour and turmoil. But there in the city are clustered together tenement and villa and palace, market and hall and house of prayer. It is representative of the social life of man, which is the very life's blood of the soul.

It is in the city that not only man's social, but his creative instincts find free play. The roaring loom and forge are there: the places of barter and exchange. There the great works of art are gathered. There the soaring architec-

Jesus the Citizen

tural triumphs are built, and the great Cathedral pile lifts its columns and arches of aspiration and prayer. There, too, men deliberate and plan for order and good government. The country youth coming up to the city as student or apprentice absorbs its wonders. And though there is much in modern city life to deaden the instinct of the soul for beauty, yet if he makes right use of its open doors to wonder, he cannot but go back to the country with an eye educated and alert to appreciate more fully the glories of nature. Having looked at her through the selective eyes of the great artist, he can look with new appreciation on the landscapes God has made. Having worshipped in the great Cathedral throng, he knows the inspiration that comes from fellowship in worship, and can bring a new meaning to the offerings of prayer and praise in quiet country places.

Even so Jesus was drawn to the city; and He was not impervious to the impressions which city life made upon Him. In His early pilgrim days, He carried back from His Father's house in the holy city abiding thoughts of aspiration and service. And He spent Himself on the city. It was a city crowd He summoned when He

Jesus and the City of God

called the weary and the heavy-laden unto Him. He would fain have spread the protecting care and pity of His great experience of God over the city, as a hen gathereth her brood beneath her wings. And towards the end, when He thought of the rewards of faithful service in the Kingdom, He thought of it in terms of rulership over cities. Thus the conception of the city was not wholly alien to His mind in His thought of the Kingdom of Heaven. He seems to picture it in the parable of the Talents as a place of many cities. For, like the city, the Kingdom is a fellowship of the closest and most intimate kind, in which men come together to further a common life, pursuing ends which converge upon the good of the whole.

Why then is it that Jesus in the main fought so shy of the conception of the city? Surely there was something in the actual reality of the city, as He knew it, that repelled Him. There can be no doubt that He felt cramped in the life of the town. We can trace in His movements an evident aversion from spending the night within walled places. Especially in Passion Week we see Him leaving the city night after night for Bethany or Olivet. He was essentially a man

Jesus the Citizen

of open spaces. He loved the open sky and the open fields. He sought the hill-tops in His hours of prayer. No doubt He recognized that, if man had made the city after the image and reflection of his own soul, he had reproduced in it also the evil that lies in his soul. Because there is a slum in the unregenerate heart of man, that is reflected also in the heart of the cities he builds.

The corporate traffickings of the city are but a reflex of the inner scheming for self. And all the gaiety of the city is just the inner life of sense writ large. Moreover, there is a big element of city life supremely indifferent to the higher life of the soul, because man, on one side of his nature, is so materialistic in his outlook. That is why the city cast Christ out at last. Nazareth rejected Him: Capernaum, Chorazin, Bethsaida treated Him for a little as an object of idle curiosity, and then despised Him: the holy city crucified Him. There was some fundamental antagonism between the life of Jesus and the life of the city. He stood for things that were eternal—immortal Truth, immortal Love, immortal Beauty, immortal Duty, and the immortal soul. And He seemed to see in the city some-

Jesus and the City of God

thing that was impermanent and transient. The eternal processes of the seasons appealed to Him more. Therefore it was that He chose His figures for the Kingdom from the life of the fields.

But we have this one hint of citizenship in the perfected Kingdom. The servant is to be made ruler over five cities or two cities in proportion to his faithfulness to the talents entrusted to his charge. The idea of the city here must not be unduly pressed. But behind Jesus' conception of rulership in the city lies the supreme principle of the Kingdom He depicted. And it betrays no likeness to man's dream of rulership. What has man's dream been?

The dream which has been most effectively established in human society for many centuries is that of an order in which some few are born to rule and the rest to serve. For men are not born equal: there are many different kinds and degrees of capacity. And out of that fact has grown the distinction between rulership and service. It has in different ages taken different forms.

The feudal system was one form, in which there came to be recognized an aristocracy of

Jesus the Citizen

birth, and a hereditary ruling class. That régime has slowly passed away: the remnants of it seem to be dying a natural death. Man is not entitled to claim any prerogative by birth to lord it over his fellowmen. For men are at least born with certain equal rights. And to be born of noble parents, or even of parents with a high degree of capacity, gives no guarantee that the nobility or the capacity will be continued. This conception of hereditary rulership has no kinship with Jesus' principle of the Kingdom.

There is again an aristocracy of intellect. But while that is very real in the realm of scientific and philosophic thought, and in the realm of imagination, it has only to a limited extent become actual in the sphere of rulership. Though in Parliaments and councils the man of outstanding intellectual gifts has often held offices of state, yet Plato's dream that the philosopher should be king has hardly ever, save in isolated and accidental instances, received concrete embodiment. In such an order there is no warrant that the man of intellectual capacity must necessarily be a just and righteous ruler. And in Jesus' conception there is a higher criterion than intellect, namely character, moral faithfulness.

Jesus and the City of God

In our day we think rather of an aristocracy of wealth and a dictatorship of vested interests. The man who has exercised his talents in acquiring money has come to be the man in whom power and rulership are invested. We are not without signs that this régime also is destined to pass away. There can, indeed, be no doubt that this distinction between rulership and service, which runs through all these types of aristocracy, is quite contrary to the Law of the Kingdom of Heaven as laid down by Jesus. What Jesus seeks to establish is an aristocracy of conscience. The Law as laid down by Jesus is that the greatest must be he that serves: not he that has the million for his servants, but he that serves the million. Rulership, to Jesus, is not to be like that of the Gentiles, whose kings lord it over them and get the title 'Benefactor.' The rulership over many cities predicted by Jesus for the faithful servant must really be identical with the utmost service.

The servant is King! Such might be said to be the Law enunciated by Jesus for His Kingdom. But this, in our day, has been perverted into another of humanity's bad dreams—communism, the dictatorship of the proletariat.

Jesus the Citizen

The serf must assume the position of ruler. Such is the claim of this new doctrine which is so assiduously being preached to-day. It still maintains the old false distinction between rulership and service. Only it claims that the tables should be overturned: and that he who formerly was held thrall in serfdom must now assert himself and win dictatorship over all other classes in the community. It is a perversion of the Christian Law of service. Because of its superficial resemblance it has rightly been called a form of anti-Christ. It refuses to recognize the higher moral sanctions. " Religion," according to Karl Marx, " is the opium of the people." God is an unnecessary hypothesis. Yet in the intensity with which it has been held and propagated, it might be said to be a new religion—though a materialistic religion, a religion for this earth only.

But the dream which Jesus had of the city of God was a dream in which the false antithesis between rulership and service is transcended. His principle was not so much that the servant should be king, as that the king should be servant. Moral authority in the celestial city is to be acquired in proportion to the quality of the service

Jesus and the City of God

rendered. In the Kingdom, whether here or beyond the sphere of earth, the greatest is he who renders the greatest amount of lowliest and most faithful service. This is the true ideal of democracy, in which each finds his vocation and niche, from which he renders service for the good of the whole. And he is rewarded, according to his faithfulness, not with a rulership which displaces service, but with a rulership which itself implies more service. This cuts across all other forms of aristocracy. The true aristocracy is the aristocracy of service, in other words, the aristocracy of conscience.

In the Book of the Revelation this dream of Christ's becomes the dream of a heavenly city. It is conceived in all the poetry of the early Church's religious fervour. Yet behind the details we can trace these same principles of Jesus. There is to be " a new heaven and a new earth "; and from out heaven itself is to come " the new Jerusalem." It is to plant itself firmly on the earth, pushing its ramparts across all the marches and frontiers of the world. It is more a thing of the future than of the present, in view of the writer of the Revelation. Jesus had compared the Kingdom rather to a tree,

Jesus the Citizen

which roots itself here and now in the earth, and which is to grow towards a glorious consummation. But in the one vision as in the other, the Kingdom is to be finally realized as perfected in the unseen heavenly realm.

'And He that sits upon the throne says, Behold I make all things new. I am Alpha and Omega, the beginning and the end.' That is to say, I am the supreme embodiment of the Kingdom's Law. I am the supreme ruler because the chief servant. "He that overcometh shall inherit all things: and I will be his God, and he shall be my son." It is to be a case of like ruler like servant. And the ways into this city are to front all the quarters of the world. Many kinds of experience are to lead men into it. Again it is to have no place set apart for worship, no temple where men might meet for praise and prayer apart from service. Service and worship have become one, for "the Lord God Almighty and the Lamb are the temple of it." When all men dwell in love, labouring in mutual service, all will dwell in the manifest presence of God. For the glory of the Lord is to lighten it, and the Lamb to be the light thereof. Once more, the kings of the earth are

Jesus and the City of God

to bring their glory and honour into it—to be absorbed and lost in the one eternal glory of service. So also shall be brought the glory and honour of the nations into it. And "His servants shall serve Him, and they shall see His face, and His name shall be written in their foreheads." That is to say, service is the condition of vision and of consecration. For service rendered unto the many is service rendered unto God.

The grandeur of this vision lacks to some extent the more intimate and tender features of Jesus' conception. There is one passage in the Fourth Gospel which we would fain claim as the *ipsissima verba* of Jesus. In it He seems to use this figure of a city, all coloured with a warm glow which it does not have elsewhere in the New Testament. "In my Father's house are many mansions," said Jesus—many resting-places or places of sojourn. 'House' here stands for the whole universe conceived of as a city which is the dwelling-place of God—the homestead, or *Heimat* of God. Papias seems to have drawn a curious distinction between Heaven, Paradise, and the City, to which the hundred-fold, the sixty-fold, and the thirty-fold followers

Jesus the Citizen

of Jesus go respectively. But here according to Jesus the various grades are all within the City, which is all-embracing. This City of God makes room for many differing types of experience, room for varying degrees of experience, room for school-rooms for incomplete souls. Jesus conceives of the pilgrimage, begun on earth—for this world is already within the house of many mansions—as a pilgrimage which is to go on and on in the Unseen World towards the radiant Heart of the Eternal. The City of God is a place of eternal progress.

And this implies that there is a sense in which the celestial city can never anywhere be realized either in time or in eternity, save only in the mind of God Himself. Every man has his vocation to fulfil in the Kingdom, and no doubt in so far as he fulfils it, he does in a measure actualize the Kingdom in himself. Yet the Kingdom must in every finite mind be of the nature of an ideal goal towards which he is striving, something as yet unrealized in its completeness. The society of the heavenly city must ever remain a society of finite souls under the One Infinite Oversoul. While the goal of our finitude may in a sense be said to be the becoming divested of finitude,

Jesus and the City of God

yet it can never, even in heaven, save in some abiding mystical vision, be fully accomplished. No citizen can become as God. Even the Son must ultimately hand over the Kingdom to the Father, that He may be All in All.

Because love is to remain the supreme reality in the city of God, the finite objects God made to love and be loved by are not to be completely lost in any mystical union, however intimate that may be, but are to remain so as to form a true communion of souls. It is to be for ever the "Father's House." And that word 'house' signifies that the perfected city of God is to realize the ideal of the family, the household, of which Christ shall say, "Whosoever shall do the will of God, the same is my brother, and my sister, and mother."

BY THE SAME AUTHOR

THE SPIRITUAL PILGRIMAGE OF JESUS

Fifth Impression   Crown 8vo, cloth boards, 6s net

" It is in many ways a remarkable book   No one can read it without being deeply impressed by the profound insight it shows both in its presentation of the development of the mind and spirit of Jesus and in its illuminating exposition of the great Gospel passages and events "—*Westminster Gazette*

" This study of the Master from a new angle of vision will prove as refreshing as it is reverent and suggestive "—*Glasgow Herald.*

" Professor Robertson's lectures have a great value in making more clear in a thousand ways the personality of Jesus, and further in giving a portrait which is full of character to the reverent reader."—*Western Morning News*

" Professor Robertson brings to his task the essential qualification—a rare kind of spiritual sympathy and penetrative insight   We may hope that this fine book is but the first of many with which this gifted writer will enrich the religious literature of our time."—*United Free Church Record.*

" This notable and beautiful work, rich and suggestive   . . No one can read it without feeling that it constitutes one of the most living of recent contributions to Christological literature."
—*Dundee Advertiser*

LONDON :
JAMES CLARKE & CO , LTD , 9 Essex St , Strand, W C

BY THE SAME AUTHOR

THE HIDDEN ROMANCE OF THE NEW TESTAMENT

Fourth Impression. Crown 8vo, cloth boards, 6s. net.

" In this volume we have the same qualities that carried the writer's former book, " The Spiritual Pilgrimage of Jesus " into immediate fame—scholarship vivified by imaginative insight, and used with an unerring sense of literary values and of human predilections The reader must have a very jaded taste who does not enjoy this book."—*The Scotsman*

" It is a piece of historical reconstruction at once imaginative and scholarly—a study in the background of the New Testament replete with human interest and spiritual suggestion The outstanding impression left by the book is that of rare imaginative genius, wedded to specialised knowledge "—*Church Family Newspaper.*

" The book is a charming example in a style of handling for which there is both need and opportunity."—*Methodist Recorder*

" Professor Robertson is to be congratulated on the appearance of a volume at once lucid, profound and suggestive, which cannot fail to receive a warm welcome."—*Edinburgh Evening News.*

" The power to bring out of so familiar a book so much constructive truth, and so many probabilities, seems to me an evidence of genius It seems like an imaginative artist and a scientific explorer working hand in hand on the early Christian literature. The book must fascinate every reader, and readers will multiply as years go on."—The Rev. R. F. HORTON, M.A., D.D.

LONDON ·
JAMES CLARKE & CO, LTD, 9 Essex St, Strand, W C 2

BY THE SAME AUTHOR

DIVINE VOCATION IN HUMAN LIFE

Crown 8vo, cloth boards, 6s. net

"The book is a scholarly and devout inquiry into a subject that concerns both mystical and experimental theology"—*The Times Literary Supplement*

"Professor Robertson develops his theme with an arresting warmth of feeling and fertility of illustration. The book is one which should be widely read"—*The Scotsman*

"It is needless to say that, like all his other work, this new book is characterized by a refinement of both style and thought which makes it a constant pleasure to read"—*Expository Times*

CONCERNING THE SOUL

Crown 8vo, cloth boards, 6s. net

"The treatment is so lucid and vivid that even the reader who is little inclined to philosophic thought will find them of absorbing interest, while to preachers and teachers who appreciate intellectual keenness and spiritual insight they will constitute a veritable mine of suggestive matter"—*The Scotsman*

"The same qualities which have charmed readers of Dr Robertson's earlier books shine forth here"—*Methodist Recorder*

"It is a masterly discussion of soul problems treated in a simple, popular manner, which adds immensely to its interest and value"—*Edinburgh Evening News*

LONDON
JAMES CLARKE & Co., Ltd., 9 Essex Street, Strand, W.C. 2

www.ingramcontent.com/pod-product-compliance
Lightning Source LLC
Chambersburg PA
CBHW072131160426
43197CB00012B/2070